The Story of the Hooked Rugs of Chéticamp and Their Artisans

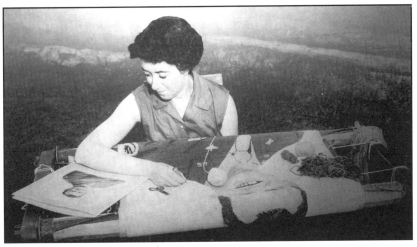

Élizabeth Lefort, the Élizabeth Lefort Gallery, Les Trois Pignons

The Story
of the
Hooked Rugs
of Chéticamp

and Their Artisans

Edited by Father Anselme Chiasson

Researched by Annie-Rose Deveau

Translated by Marcel LeBlanc

BRETON BOOKS

La Société Saint-Pierre wishes to sincerely thank the following people: Annie-Rose Deveau, researcher; Father Anselme Chiasson, editor; Marcel LeBlanc, translator; Gilles Deveau, drawings; Ephrem Boudreau, proofreading and rewriting of the original edition; Sr. Rita Poirier; Father Charles Aucoin. Very special thanks are extended to the many people of the region for their collaboration either through information supplied and/or for photographs submitted. Editor of the revised edition: Ronald Caplan, with Bonnie Thompson, production assistant. We also thank the following people for their help with the revised edition: Donald Deschênes for "Tribute to Father Anselme Chiasson"; and Yvette Aucoin, Lisette Bourgeois, Ida LeLièvre, Lorraine Roach, and Charles D. Roach, all from La Société Saint-Pierre.

The photo of Mabel Bell is from the family collections of Alexander Graham Bell, Library of Congress, Prints and Photographs Division.

Cover photo of Jacqueline Larade Burton, employee of La Société Saint-Pierre, was taken at Flora's Gift Shop by Daniel Aucoin. Photos on the back cover: Les Trois Pignons, by Warren Gordon; The Tree of Life, La Sagouine, Jesus the Adolescent—photos of tapestries at the Élizabeth Lefort Gallery, at Les Trois Pignons.

The "Tribute to Miss Lillian Burke" (originally called "Cape Breton's Debt to Lillian Burke") was first published by the Halifax Department of Industry and Commerce in its October 1952 issue of *Handcrafts*. This article contributed to the revival of the history of the hooked rug and, most importantly, it succeeded in creating an awareness of Miss Burke's role in the Chéticamp hooked rug industry. The "Tribute to Father Anselme Chiasson" is taken from Donald Deschênes' preface to *Contes de Chéticamp*, translated by Rosie Aucoin Grace in *Acadian Tales from Cape Breton Island* (Breton Books).

 Canada Council   Conseil des Arts
for the Arts   du Canada
We acknowledge the support of the
Canada Council for the Arts for our publishing program.

We also acknowledge support from Cultural Affairs,
Nova Scotia Department of Tourism and Culture.

We acknowledge the financial support of the Government of Canada
through the Book Publishing Industry Development Program (BPIDP)
for our publishing activities. Canadä

Library and Archives Canada Cataloguing in Publication

The story of the hooked rugs of Chéticamp and their artisans / edited by Anselme Chiasson; researched by Annie-Rose Deveau; translated by Marcel LeBlanc. — Rev. ed.

Previous ed. titled: The history of Chéticamp hooked rugs and their artisans.

Translation of: L'histoire des tapis hookés de Chéticamp et de leurs artisans.

ISBN 1-895415-75-6

1. Rugs, Hooked—Nova Scotia—Chéticamp—History. I. Chiasson, Anselme, 1911-2004. II. Deveau, Annie-Rose. III. LeBlanc, Marcel, 1941-   .

TT850.H5713 2006   746.7'40971691   C2006-901924-X

Printed in Canada

TABLE OF CONTENTS

Foreword *vii*

1 Chéticamp: Its Geographic Location
   and Its Founding and Evolution *1*

2 Different Kinds of Rugs and Their Use *4*
   Défaisure rugs, braided rugs, catalognes,
   rosette rugs, *breillon* rugs. Use of rugs.

3 Rugs Made with Wool and Jute Canvas
   with the Use of a Hook *8*
   Their nature. Instruments or tools. The materials:
   a) the canvas, b) the wool. How they are made.
   Origins of these rugs.

4 The First Sales: The Pedlars *23*

5 Fledgling Beginnings,
   with Different Kinds of Rugs *26*
   Various materials. At Mick Boudreau's.
   At Moïse Aucoin's. At the MacFarlands'.
   Covers used in sleighs.

6 Important Turning Point in
   the History of Hooked Rugs:
   The Arrival of Miss Lillian Burke *34*
   Alexander Graham Bell's family. Arrival of Miss
   Lillian Burke. Their arrival in Chéticamp. Mrs.
   Marie-Jane Doucet, Miss Burke's agent. Changing
   aspects of the rugs. The dyes. Sulfuric acid.

7 Miss Burke's Demands
   and Her Kindheartedness *45*

8 The Extraordinary Development
   of the Rug Making Industry *53*
   Mrs. Luce (à Charlie à Polite) Deveau. Mrs. Annie
   (à Joseph à Jean) Chiasson. At Placide (à Lubin)
   Boudreau's. Mrs. Marie (à Joseph à Victor) Roach.
   Miss Marie-Edna Roach. Charlie Doucet. Mrs.
   Christie-Anne (à John à Raymond) Poirier. Marie-
   Yvonne and Isabelle Muise. Miss Antoinette
   Deveau.

9 **The Notorious Crisis of 1936-1937** *70*
Division among the "hookeuses." Miss Burke's last years. Mrs. Marie (à Willie à Hélène) Aucoin.

10 **Mrs. Marie (à Charlie à Lubin) Aucoin and the Dissenting Group** *75*
Difficult beginnings. A large amount of work. New markets. New momentum. The Church's rugs. The end of Mrs. Marie (à Charlie) Aucoin's business.

11 **Some of This Handcraft's Renowned Artists** *82*
Mrs. Antoinette (à Paul) Lefort. Mrs. Marguerite-Marie (à Joseph à Den) Chiasson. Mrs. Catherine (à Jos à John) Poirier. Marie and Joseph-Léo Muise. Paulite (à Paddée) and Sadie Roach. Mrs. Marie-Stella (à Louis-Léo) Bourgeois. Mrs. Élizabeth Lefort-Hansford. Annie-Rose and Gérard Deveau. Other personalities. Mrs. Marie-Louise Cormier. Mrs. Luce-Marie Boudreau.

12 **The Boutiques** *120*
The Acadian Inn Restaurant. Marie LeLièvre's Hooked Rugs Boutique. Le Foyer du souvenir. Flora's Boutique. La Coopérative artisanale de Chéticamp ltée. Edna's Gift Shop. Hooked Rugs of Clothilde and Henri Bourgeois. Jean's Gift Shop. Bella Poirier's Hooked Rugs. The Acadian Lighthouse. Le Gabion. Chéticamp's Gift Shop.

13 **New Initiatives and Perspectives for the Future** *135*
Rug making kits. Courses on how to hook rugs. New horizons. Jamac Creations. Projects aimed at producing larger rugs. Project for a workshop on how to dye wool. The Élizabeth Lefort Gallery.

Conclusion *145*

Tribute to Miss Lillian Burke *147*

Tribute to Father Anselme Chiasson *149*

COLOUR PHOTOS BETWEEN PAGES *56* AND *57*

Foreword

Handcrafts in the Maritime Provinces have experienced a newfound popularity.

Hooked rugs and tapestries have been famous for more than 55 years and constitute a unique form of handcrafts in Chéticamp. These are renowned for their perfect workmanship, rich soft colours, their diversity of design, and often also for their distinguished owners.

These rugs have an equally colourful history. The fact that they were introduced in Chéticamp by a New York artist, Miss Lillian Burke, and by the family of the famous telephone inventor, Mr. Alexander Graham Bell, already gives them an illustrious beginning. The evolution of these rugs to their present high-quality workmanship, their economic importance to the area, the social activity which was and still is associated with this form of handcrafts, and the fame of several artists in this medium, all required that the history of these rugs be recorded.

La Société Saint-Pierre, cultural society of the Acadians of Cape Breton, with its headquarters in Chéticamp, rightfully initiated the project. The task of researching the historical facts was entrusted to Mrs. Annie-Rose (à Gérard) Deveau, a lady of many talents and especially competent in this kind of handcrafts.

During four years, Mrs. Deveau diligently researched the facts. She consulted older people, such as Mrs. Conrad Fiset, who at one hundred years of age still made rugs. She also consulted the persons responsible for rendering this form of handcraft into a respectable one, as well as those who played a role in making it the important industry which it is today. She recorded accounts of the type of social activity which the making of these rugs entailed, especially the larger ones whose fabrication required the simultaneous efforts of several people.

The research associated with this history proved to be difficult. The birth of this form of handcraft, its development and its eventual high-quality workmanship covered a half century, and the evolutionary facts of this history were never recorded by anybody in Chéticamp. Of course, certain non-local newspapers reported some important events, for example the presentation of one of these rugs to a renowned person such as the Queen of England, one of the Presidents of the United States of America or one of the Prime Ministers. Unfortunately, the newspaper clippings relating these events, which were found in various homes, had been cut out with neither the name of the newspaper nor the date of publication having been recorded.

At the beginning, as we will see later, Miss Lillian Burke bought all the rugs through a woman who was her representative in Chéticamp. However, around 1936-1937 an important group broke away from the artist's monopoly and with its newfound wings flew in its own direction. This split caused some friction and bitterness, traces of which have not been erased from some memories. Consequently, some people who could have been a valuable source of information were reticent; others, not understanding the importance of this research nor the importance of publishing a book on the subject, when asked, refused to supply information about their own work.

These people as well as others whom we will most likely forget to mention will probably be disappointed not to find their names within these pages. Understandably, it was impossible to mention the names of all the people who have made beautiful rugs over a period of more than fifty years.

It was necessary to mention the persons and groups which were representative of the history, the social aspects and all other facets of this type of handcraft.

The coloured photographs cannot reproduce faithfully the hundreds of shades of colour which can be found in certain tapestries; however, they are a fairly close representation of the actual thing. Gilles Deveau's illustrations help in understanding the difficult descriptions of the tools used as well as the actual fabrication of the rugs.

Finally, as the editor appointed by La Société Saint-Pierre, I had to extract from the reams of historical notes gathered by Mrs. Annie-Rose Deveau through her diligent research, the "very substance" of this book.

This history of the rugs and tapestries of Chéticamp, which up to now was only superficially known and which became our task to amplify through research and writing, really captivated the researcher and myself. It will just as surely interest the reader.

Father Anselme Chiasson, O.F.M., Capuchin

CHAPTER 1

Chéticamp:
Its Geographic Location
and Its Founding
and Evolution

The village of Chéticamp is located on the west coast of Cape Breton in Nova Scotia. Its population numbers 3,500—all, with a few exceptions, Acadians.

The place was visited by European, Basque and other fishermen long before Jacques Cartier discovered Canada. These fishermen used to dry their cod on the shore of La Pointe. However, there was no permanent settlement there before the end of the 18th century.

It was also at La Pointe de l'Île (presqu'île) of Chéticamp that the merchant from Jersey Island, Charles Robin, set up his fishing post in 1767. This attracted permanent settlers.

The first Acadians to settle in Chéticamp in 1782 were Pierre Bois and Joseph Richard, also known as Matinal. Soon other Acadians arrived, about 20 with their families, all victims of the dispersion of 1755. The list of names of the first settlers, to which others were added later, is as follows: Aucoin,

Boudreau, Bourgeois, Chiasson, Cormier, Deveau, Doucet, Gaudet, LeBlanc, Maillet, Poirier, and Roach.

They cultivated a plot of land to meet their needs for meat and vegetables. But above all they were fishermen, fishing to be able to provide for themselves from Robin's store the items which they could not fabricate or the food which they could not grow.

For almost a century, the Robins were the only fish buyers and merchants in the area. The people of Chéticamp became subservient to them and were kept in extreme poverty.

Only with the advent of the cooperative movement in the 1930s did the people realize true economic independence and a comfortable standard of living which has steadily improved since. Fishing thrived and became profitable.

Chéticamp is one of the few Acadian villages which has had the benefit of a high school for more than a century—and that shows. It has produced professionals, priests and other professionally religious people, and especially people of initiative who have transformed the face of the parish for over 50 years. They have provided the village with various cooperative enterprises such as a general store, a fish processing plant, a Credit Union, many other active associations, a cultural centre called Les Trois Pignons, a home for the aged, a recreational centre, a hockey arena, a printing plant, community radio and television, and so forth.

With the opening of wide roads that ring Cape Breton and especially the highlands of the famous national park and Cabot Trail, the tourists come in greater and greater numbers and constitute the second source of revenue for Chéticamp, after the fishing industry.

Chéticamp is renowned for the magnificence of its landscapes, the old melodious language of its inhabitants, and for a rich folkloric heritage.[1] Chéticamp, however, is becoming more and more known, even at the international level, for its handcrafts that have become very specialized in one area—the hooked rug[2]—which has become an art form.

2

The residents of Chéticamp did not arrive at perfection in this form of handcraft overnight. The evolutionary process which led to high-quality workmanship and product in itself constitutes a history rich in human and social elements. At the same time it is a marvelous story of a gradual but constant progress in an art form which is particular to this Acadian region.

However, Chéticamp folks were fabricating various other kinds of rugs long before the present art form surfaced. We will briefly describe these variations before we fully immerse ourselves into the chapter "Rugs Made with Wool and Jute Canvas...."

1. See *Chéticamp: histoire et traditions acadiennes*, by Anselme Chiasson, éd. des Aboiteaux, Moncton, New Brunswick, 1961; Breton Books, Wreck Cove, Nova Scotia, 2003; translated as *Chéticamp: History and Acadian Traditions*, Breakwater Books, St. John's, Newfoundland, 1986; Breton Books, Wreck Cove, N.S., 1998; and eleven volumes of folk songs from Chéticamp, entitled *Chansons d'Acadie*, over 560 songs in all.

2. It seems that the French language does not have an appropriate term to describe this kind of rug made with a hook—these are called very appropriately in English "hooked rugs." The people from Québec use the term *crocheter*, *tapis crochetés* (Jocelyne Mathieu. *Faire des tapis à la mode de l'île d'Orléans*, Éditions Jean Basile, Montréal, 1980). However, by consulting a dictionary, it becomes apparent that the term is not applicable to rugs made with wool and jute canvas. The people of Chéticamp have therefore originated a word, taken from English "to hook," and they have given it its own particular Anglicized pronounciation of *hooker* (pronounced *ouquer*). The words *hooké, hookeuses, hookeur, hookage* are derivatives of the infinitive form *hooker*. This term is indigenous to Chéticamp as are the rugs which are the subject matter of this book.

CHAPTER 2

Different Kinds of Rugs and Their Use

In Chéticamp, as everywhere else no doubt, the cold floors especially in winter encouraged women to make rugs in order to protect their feet from the cold and be more comfortable.

In response to an obvious need, the Acadian women had to have been making rugs as far back as the earliest days of Acadia and they must have brought with them from France the technique of rug making, even though the unfortunate events of our history have deprived us of the documents necessary to support this contention.

The oldest kinds of rugs remembered to this day in Chéticamp are those made with *défaisures*, braided rugs, woven rugs, rosette rugs and rugs made out of *breillons*.

Rugs made with *défaisures*[1]

The rug made with *défaisures* is one of the oldest forms of rugs known in Chéticamp. To make them, the women used old woolen clothes such as sweaters, mittens and socks. These woolen fabrics of various colours were cut into strips of about 2 inches[2] in width. The entire lengths of these fabric strips were then frayed.

These strips were sewn in close rows on a jute canvas. They

4

were sewn in such a way that the frayed side was visible and the rug thus fashioned took on a velvety texture. Each frayed strip was of a different colour, which resulted in a very colourful and beautiful rug. Another equally beautiful effect was achieved by arranging these strips in the form of squares.

These rugs were very beautiful and were used by the bedside. Their only fault was that they were great dust gatherers.

Braided rugs

The term "braided" spells out very well the kind of rug this is. Here is how they were made. First, long strips of used fabrics were cut, about an inch in width and of different colours. Three of these strips were braided together, the length of the braid varying according to the desired size for the rug. This braid, rolled on itself to form a flat plane, was sewed with special care being taken that it would lay flat on the floor and would not show any bumps.

Today, these large braided rugs are the pride and joy of the people who use them to cover the floor of their very fashionable living rooms. In the past, they were placed at the entrance of the house where the people used them as mats to wipe their feet upon entering.

The "catalognes"

"Catalognes" were woven on a loom. The same material as for braided rugs was used, that is strips cut from worn clothing and all sorts of other fabrics. In Chéticamp however, more often, two strips of "catalognes" were sewn together to form bedspreads. They saw very little use as rugs. However, when pedlars started to buy all kinds of rugs, the women separated the bedcover and sold each woven section as an individual rug.

Rosette rugs

Circles cut from worn fabrics were sewn next to each other on a piece of jute. On each of these rounds other circles of diminishing size and varying colour were superimposed resulting in a rosette. These rugs consisting of rosettes—hence their name—

of various colours and tastefully fashioned were very beautiful.

Breillon rugs

Breillon rugs were made as follows: used garments of fabrics other than wool were cut into long strips of about one half inch in width. These *breillons*, as they were called, were set by means of a hook into a canvas made from burlap bags.

The canvas, which had to be very taut, was nailed to a wooden frame which was either square or rectangular in shape. To make the rug itself, one proceeded as follows: a strip of *breillon* was held under the canvas with the left hand and, with the right hand on top of the canvas, a hook was introduced into a mesh of the canvas to draw up through the mesh a small amount of the strip to the desired height. This operation was repeated, the hook being inserted into every second or third mesh, and using one strip of *breillon* after another.

It is known that the designs of some of these *breillon* rugs featured sailboats, domestic animals, birds, trees, etc. It appears that there are no such rugs left in Chéticamp; however, in recent years this style of rug has surfaced again.

The pattern of many other rugs consisted in a geometric layout of the coloured strips on the canvas, either in simple squares or rectangles of various colours in imitation brickwork. Another pattern was achieved by hooking always in a horizontal direction changing colour every time a new strip was used thus giving the rug a many-coloured look. Some rugs are still hooked in this fashion in Chéticamp but much less often than before.

Use of rugs

Before getting to the heart of the matter of this book, woolen rugs hooked on canvas, which from now on will be called hooked rugs, let us examine briefly the use of these rugs.

Before Chéticamp was blessed with electricity which was supplied in 1937, the houses were heated with wood-burning stoves. In the winter the floors were always cold. This was especially noticeable when one moved only a short distance away from the stove. Wall-to-wall carpets sold in modern-day stores had not been heard of yet. However, in quite a few houses *breillon* or braided rugs covered a part of the floor in all the rooms. This was their practical use.

Some of these rosette or *breillon* rugs, and especially later hooked rugs, were very beautiful. Sometimes the most beautiful ones were set aside for special occasions. Consequently, some people only took out their most beautiful rugs for special holidays or when they received important visitors such as the parish priest during his yearly visit. As a gesture to demonstrate their faith, some people donated their rugs to the church where they would be laid in front of the main altar.

In the past all the rugs had a practical use while a decorative purpose was not necessarily excluded. While it is true that some hooked rugs still have a practical use, due to the evolution in their workmanship and due to the demand for them on the North American market, Chéticamp rugs have become high quality, decorative and artistic works.

In this small village of 3,500 inhabitants, each year rugs are sold for a value of about half a million dollars. The commercial aspect of these rugs does not detract from their artistic value, for their main *raison d'etre* is their beauty. On the contrary, the business aspect associated with these rugs motivates their producers to strive for excellence. The rugs, large and small, which were meant to cover floors, have evolved into tapestries and murals, some of which are works of art.

Finally, in most homes of Chéticamp, the owners proudly keep a few of their most beautiful hooked rugs, which usually sport a floral motif for the floor or adorn the walls with a landscape or multi-coloured birds.

1. *Défaisures.* From the verb *défaire.* A piece of knitted woolen fabric was cut up and the result was *défaisures.* In Chéticamp this term is pronounced *éfaisures* by most people.
2. Canada having adopted the metric system relatively recently, the rugs were measured according to the British system of inches, feet and square feet, and the weight measures are in ounces and pounds.

CHAPTER 3

Rugs Made with Wool and Jute Canvas with the Use of a Hook

The nature of hooked rugs

Woolen hooked rugs are made by the same procedure as *breillon* rugs, but they have a much more delicate and fine structure. These rugs are particularly well suited for the creation of different motifs expressed in many varied colours; in short, artistic creations.

The beauty of these rugs, besides the choice of design and the blend of colours, is the result of skillfully drawing the wool through the mesh in such a way that each stitch is equal in height so that the rug has a uniform and smooth surface without any rough patches.

The production of one of these rugs requires special instruments or tools, particular fabrics and dyes. In fact, it is an artistic craft.

Instruments or tools

These rugs can only be made on a canvas which is stretched tightly. For this purpose, a wooden frame to which the canvas is attached securely is required.

For small rugs, about one square foot or somewhat larger, a small fixed frame without rollers on which the canvas can be stretched can be used.

These frames can be installed on legs or they can rest on

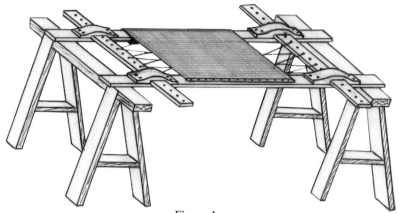

Figure 1
In the earlier days, frames without rollers were used

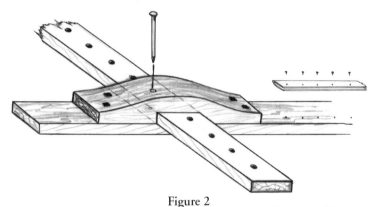

Figure 2
This sketch shows how the canvas was set up on this type of frame.

the backs of two chairs. Rugs of a greater size require a bigger frame with rollers. The frame is made of solid wood and rests on four legs. They are about two and a half feet high, which is a suitable height for a person working while sitting. The width of these frames varies with the width of the rug to be produced. Different widths of rugs can be produced on a particular frame but no rug can be wider than the frame itself. A roller in front and one in the back, at the same level as the frame, make it

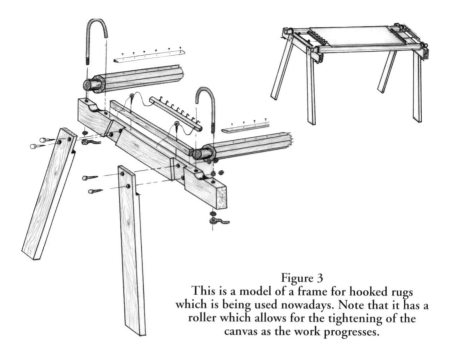

Figure 3
This is a model of a frame for hooked rugs
which is being used nowadays. Note that it has a
roller which allows for the tightening of the
canvas as the work progresses.

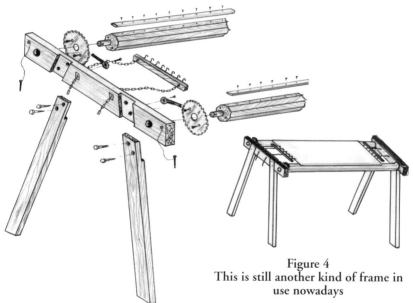

Figure 4
This is still another kind of frame in
use nowadays

possible to produce a rug from two and a half feet long to any
other length desired.

The canvas is rolled tightly on the back roller and is then

brought forward to the front roller where it is attached securely. Besides conveniently rolling up the rug, these rollers are necessary to keep the canvas taut, a condition which is necessary for the finished product to be well executed. *[See Figures 3 and 4.]*

Two rollers are sufficient for rugs which will be hooked from the front of the frame. In the case of large rugs on which eight to ten people will be working, the frame has to be much larger to allow them to work at the same time, both at the front and at the back of the frame. These large rugs produced on large frames require five rollers: one in front, one in back, two in the middle at the same level as the other two and almost touching each other, and the fifth below these two middle rollers and much lower. With this kind of frame, one half of the canvas is rolled on the first roller and the other half on the back roller so that the centre of the canvas is stretched between the two. When this part of the canvas is "hooked" it is slackened and passed between the two rollers and attached to the bottom one. This roller has a slot and tongue which secure the rug and allow it to be rolled tightly. The part of the canvas which is thus stretched by the rollers is worked on.

The front, back, and bottom rollers have a special mechanism which prevent them from turning in the opposite direction, thereby keeping the canvas tightly stretched. This mechanism can be a rack and pinion, or it can be a hole in the end of the roller and in the framework in which a big nail or steel rod is inserted. Another such mechanism which is more practical has been invented: a steel rod which has been bent to fit around the two ends of the rollers fits in a hole in the framework and is tightened underneath the framework by means of nuts thus anchoring the roller in the desired position. *[See Figure 5.]*

The front and back rollers are covered with a canvas to which the canvas to be "hooked" is sewn with strong thread. In the case of small rugs of about a square foot, the canvas can be nailed directly to the small frame.

11

The tool used to "hook" the rug is a straight hook which is homemade. It is made by driving a two-inch nail one and a half inches into a two-inch block of wood. The head of the nail is then cut off and the end of the nail showing is filed to a point in which a notch is made. Finally, the block of wood is fashioned into a smooth and manageable handle, rounded out and thinned towards the nail. *[See Figure 6.]*

Before starting a hooked rug, a design has to be applied to the canvas. In earlier days, a stick which had been dipped in indelible ink was used. Nowadays felt markers are used.

The designs are drawn on the canvas before it is set up on the frame. The drawing is done with the canvas lying on the

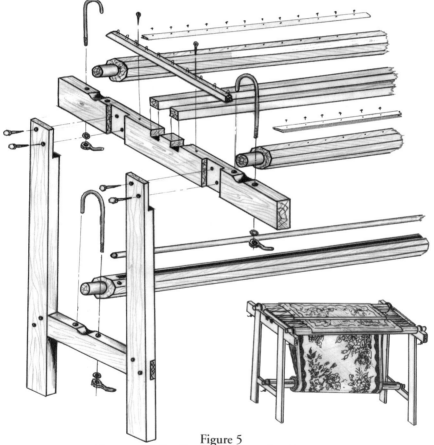

Figure 5
Frame with 5 rollers used to produce large rugs,
as was done in the past in Chéticamp

  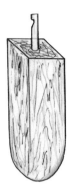 

Figure 6
This figure shows the progressive steps in fashioning a hook for
making rugs

table, or on the floor if the rug is to be very big. One exception to this would be designs for coasters or small centrepieces which are round in shape. The coasters usually measure three inches in diameter and the centrepieces around fourteen inches. For coasters and centrepieces, the canvas is first stretched on the frame and several coasters or centrepieces are drawn on the canvas with enough space separating them so that when they are cut from the canvas it will be possible to sew the canvas underneath thus blocking the finished product. *[See Figure 7.]*

The materials
a) *The canvas*

The foundation material for the rugs is jute canvas.

When rug making started in Chéticamp, women used potato or bran bags or sacks. Very early on, however, jute canvas had to be ordered from factories so that larger pieces and more uniform canvas would be available for making the bigger rugs. Of course, this ended the use of potato and bran sacks or bags.

In modern times, this canvas is imported in large rolls from Prince Edward Island, the Rittermere-Hurst-Field Company in Aurora, Ontario, and even directly from Scotland or Holland where it is produced.

b) *The wool*

Since the founding of Chéticamp, the majority of families tended a few sheep, sometimes for the meat but more often for the wool. In the earlier days of rug making, a lot of clothing was knitted[1] and the best wool was reserved for that purpose. The lesser quality wool which was obtained from the legs and belly of the sheep was used for rug making.[2] Eventually it was understood that quality rugs required quality wool.

As the industry of rug making progressed, more wool than could be produced by the sheep in Chéticamp was needed. It had to be obtained elsewhere such as from the Scots who lived in North East Margaree.

Amédée (à Belone) Deveau[3] started and ran the wool business for many years. He would fetch it from the Scots by means of a *caboroit* [a horse-drawn carriage with four wheels

Figure 7
A canvas has to be stamped before it is hooked

and a seat] in the summer and by sled in the winter. He bought the wool in its raw state as sheared off the sheep for ten cents a pound, and sold it in Chéticamp for fifteen. Not being able to afford to buy more than one hundred to one hundred and fifty pounds at a time, he would make frequent trips. In spite of difficulties, he managed to buy between five and six thousand pounds per year.

This wool, bought unprocessed, first had to be picked and washed carefully in order to remove lint and impurities. When this operation was finished, half of the weight of the wool remained. The wool then had to be torn into small pieces and carded. Women would gather in a particular household to do this work. These meetings were called *écharpisseries* and *écarderies*.

For a fairly long time, a few women were still carding their

Écharpisserie: Mrs. Annie Blanche Aucoin and Mrs. Agnès Lefort

wool, but as the quantity used increased, most women sent the wool to be carded by people who specialized in this activity, namely Romain Roach, from Chéticamp, Arsène (à Jean) Doucet of the neighbouring parish, and the Harts of North East Margaree, who were renowned for better quality work. The wool was brought to the carding mills by the mail carrier, who took it back when carded.

The wool was then spun, often by a group of women gathered together for that very purpose. This occasion was

A spinning bee from past years

known as a *filerie*. The wool was then skeined, dyed to the desired colour, and wound into balls. Having been thus prepared, the wool was ready to be hooked into a rug.

There was a time when they bought the wool in skeins from Condon's carding mill in Charlottetown, Prince Edward Island. Nowadays, the wool is imported from Filature Lemieux Inc., St.-Éphrem, Québec.

The history of the dyeing of the wool and the use of mordants has changed very much as the quality of rugs improved, and also with the arrival in Chéticamp in 1927 of artist Lillian Burke. Development of these two important aspects of rug making and their application will be dealt with in another chapter.

How hooked rugs are made

Once the design is stamped on the canvas and the latter installed on the frame and tightened by the rollers, the process of "hooking" a rug can begin.

The hook is held in the right hand above the canvas and a strand of wool unwound from a ball is held in the left hand

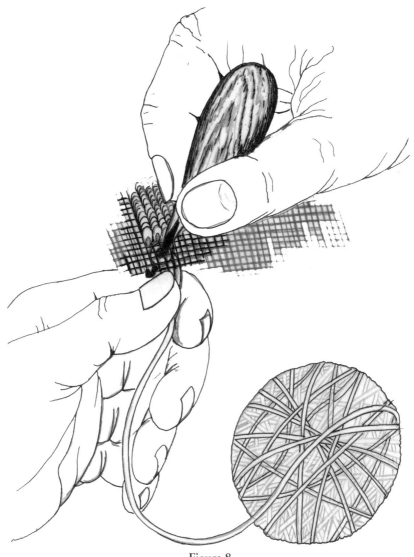

Figure 8
This drawing illustrates how a hooked rug or tapestry is made.
A small loop is made in each mesh of the canvas.

underneath the canvas. The hook is inserted in a mesh of the canvas and the left hand fixes the strand of wool on the hook. The strand is then drawn through the mesh with the hook forming a five-millimetre loop. This loop is called a stitch. This procedure is repeated in successive meshes with the person hooking the rug making sure that the stitches are of uniform size and height. *[See Figure 8.]*

The more difficult motifs to realize, because of the design and the colours, are always worked first. When it is time to change colour, the last stitch is drawn to a greater height than the others and is then snipped to the height of the other stitches. The long strand of wool is then drawn back through the canvas and underneath it; the work is continued using a strand of wool of a different colour.

According to experts in this craft, it is better to fill in the background and border by working small squares successively. The rug is hooked by starting with the border and working towards the centre.

As stated before, a strip of rug facing the worker is completed first. Then the roller is turned to bring forth another section of unworked canvas.

Much care must be taken with all the different aspects of rug making. Thus when the hooking of the rug is finished, the completion of the border on the four sides requires careful work. To ensure that the canvas would be invisible, the practice was, for a long time, to finish the border with a needle which was used to wind strands of wool of the same colour as the border, touching each other. This was a long tedious procedure which could mean a whole day's work for several women, especially in the case of large rugs. When through the course of the years it became obvious that a border thus fashioned wore out very quickly and became frayed, this method of finishing the rug was given up.

The method for finishing the border of the rug which was then tried is as follows: the border, of constant width, was folded under the rug and sewn in place; by means of a brush, the folded edge was then dyed the same colour as the border. Folding the canvas under the border is still done today but it is no longer dyed.

Finally, when the rug is finished, it has to be ironed. In the earlier days of rug making, this was done with the use of flat irons which were heated on top of a stove. If a large rug was to be ironed, this procedure turned out to be quite a chore! First the floor had to be scrubbed clean. Then a hearty fire had to be built in the stove. Several women would come to help, bringing their flat irons. Their shoes having been removed, the women would roll out the rug, and with a dampened cloth and a flat iron they would press the entire surface of the rug. This work could only be done with the women kneeling. Once the pressing of the rug was finished, it was left laid out on the floor to dry. It was then rolled up and shipped to its buyer.[4]

It is to be noted that the quality of the rugs hooked in Chéticamp has undergone a steady and progressive development. At the beginning, heavy wool which was of inferior quality was used. Then, up to the 1960s, heavy but good quality wool was used. Consequently, the hooking of the rug required a stitch in every second or third mesh of the canvas. In modern-day rug hooking, a fine quality wool and close stitching give the rug a finish which is quite superior to that of the past.

The mesh of a canvas is made by jute threads crossing each other at right angles. The problem then becomes how to draw with hook lines which are not vertical or horizontal. For example, how can one, using a hook, draw an oblique line, or the mast and shroud of a sailing ship leaning into the wind? How can a design which features curves, rounds, a leaf, a rose, a wheel, etc., be realized? In the stamping of the design, the ink is applied to the threads of the canvas as well as the meshes, but the hook can only be inserted into a square mesh of canvas. For a long time, trying to produce oblique lines and curves by means of a hook inserted in the meshes resulted in obvious zigzag work. When the coarser wool was used, however, the zigzag effect was less noticeable, but the finished product was not as refined.

The zigzag effect caused by the very nature of the canvas becomes more pronounced when finer and modern wool is used. With finer wool, the stitches are smaller and are hooked into each mesh of the canvas, thus making the zigzag effect more obvious when oblique lines or curves are attempted. Somehow, some measure which would avoid this major undesirable effect had to be found. The ingenious solution which is yet unknown to many rug hookers consisted in hooking two or three stitches of the adjacent colour into the meshes which designate the line being produced. This procedure is applied all along both sides of the line so that the intermingling colours negate the zigzag effect and allow for the production of a smooth oblique line, a curve, or a circle, according to what the pattern requires.

The preceding paragraphs have described the steady and progressive evolution of the hooked rugs produced in Chéticamp to their present high-quality workmanship.

Origins of these rugs

Unlike rugs made out of *breillons* and canvas, which were known at the beginning of Chéticamp's history, rugs hooked with wool were introduced to the village at a later date.

It appears that the woolen rug was made known in Chéticamp by the wife of Dr. Napoleon Fiset. The latter, born in Ancienne-Lorette, Québec, was the brother of Father Pierre Fiset, ordained to the priesthood in 1864 and posted to the Diocese of Antigonish. At the invitation of his brother, Dr. Fiset came to Cape Breton in 1875 to establish his practice in Chéticamp following the appointment of Father Fiset as curate of that parish.

Dr. Fiset was married to Maria Forest, an Acadian from Arichat, who had studied and boarded with the Sisters of Notre-Dame, settled in Arichat since 1855.

Maria Forest was born in 1854, and died in Chéticamp in 1937. She was a very intelligent woman and was blessed with the soul of an artist. From the nuns, who were originally from Quebec[5], she had learned how to hook rugs using wool and jute canvas. While a boarder at the convent, she had designed and hooked a magnificent rug which still exists. This rug, which is more than a century old, can be admired at the home of Mrs. Amélia (à Alphonse) Chiasson. The background was worked in needlepoint stitching, the birds and flowers were hooked

Mrs. Napoléon Fiset (Maria Forest)

in relief out of wool, and the leaves were made with beads. A masterpiece!

[See colour photo 3—colour photos between pages 56 and 57.]

1. For "knitted," the Acadians did not use the word *tricoter*, in the earlier days it was even unknown. The term used then and to this day is the old term *brocher*.

2. This wool is called *rapillons* in Chéticamp.

3. There will be many occasions where Acadian names from Chéticamp will be mentioned in this book. In order to distinguish one person who bears the same name as another, the people add the name of the father; thus Amédée (à Belone, the father) Deveau. In the case of a married woman, the name of the father is replaced by the name of her husband. Thus we have Zabine (à Jos, the husband) Chiasson. Some people were almost exclusively known by their nicknames. Very often the names are used in abbreviated or modified form such as Médée for Amédée, Polite for Hyppolyte, and Patrice is transformed into Paddée, etc. Generally this particular usage of names is adhered to in this book, as it will not distract the readers foreign to the village and will allow for the Chéticamp residents to recognize themselves.

4. It should be mentioned that large rugs were usually only produced upon the special request of a buyer. The rugs made today are not of as large dimensions

as in the past.

5.   It seems that there is a close parallel in the development of this handcraft in Chéticamp with similar developments in the Province of Québec. When the hooked rugs made before the arrival of Miss Burke are compared with the rugs hooked in Québec, the style and designs are very much alike. Cf. "The hooked Rug—its origin," by Marius Barbeau, *Mémoire et comptes rendus de la Société Royale du Canada*, Third Series, Section II, Vol. 36, 1942, Ottawa. From the same source: "The Origin of the hooked Rug," *The Magazine Antique*, August 1947, and "Hooked Rug—Its origin," from *Technique*, Industrial Publication, Vol. XVII, No. 65, Montréal, June 1942. Jocelyne Mathieu, *Faire des tapis à la mode de l'île d'Orléans*, Éditions Jean Basile, Montréal, 1980, 118 pages.

CHAPTER 4

The First Sales: The Pedlars

No doubt, the women of Chéticamp made the rugs to express their artistic talents, but primarily they made them for domestic use. This was true of the various kinds of rugs made in this area. There was absolutely no question of selling the rugs; besides, there were no buyers.

However, around 1920, pedlars started their business in Cape Breton. The names of some of them—Harry Shore, Ben Joe, Ralph and Harry Gaffin, Bill Webber and a young lady called Dean—are of Oriental, Jewish or Central European origin. At first, the people of Chéticamp called them "Arabs," then they became known as the "Jews."

These people settled in the important business centres such as Halifax, Sydney and New Waterford. From these towns and cities, they extended their business activity into the countryside, going from door to door carrying their wares with them. Their merchandise, which consisted of clothes, bed covers, dishes, watches, necklaces and many other varied items, was at first carried on their backs, but later was transported in horse-drawn carts and eventually in trucks. This merchandise, which was bought at fire or liquidation sales, was sold at prices that turned handsome profits for the pedlars.

The travelling salesmen were quick to realize that the rugs they saw in Chéticamp homes were beautiful and valuable. They started to barter some of their merchandise for the rugs. They accepted all kinds of rugs. Sly foxes that they were, these salesmen gave very little in exchange for the rugs, and then sold them in the large urban centres of Canada and even the United States. The women of Chéticamp were happy to have useful articles in exchange for their rugs which had cost them but their effort and time.

The following examples will paint a clearer picture of this bartering action. Mrs. Élizabeth (à Onésime) Muise exchanged seven rugs, each ten square feet in area, for an inexpensive winter coat. Marie Poirier and Sophie Romard exchanged two *breillon* rugs, ten square feet each and representing much work on their part, for two flannelette blankets. One woman had made a large *breillon* rug which covered the whole kitchen floor; she exchanged it for some cheap-looking linoleum. Poor her! The pedlar had the rug cleaned and sold it for $600. When word of such bargains spread, these merchants arrived in the spring with truck loads of linoleum which they exchanged for rugs.

In this era (1920-1940), the people of Chéticamp understood very little English and most did not speak it at all. Before highways were built ushering in the era of tourism, with the exception of a few salesmen who visited the local merchants, strangers were a rare sight in Chéticamp. It is also true that when these pedlars who spoke only English arrived at the homes, the women were rather scared of them.

One woman from the neighbouring parish, in the process of spring cleaning, had washed one of her beautiful rugs and had hung it to dry outside on the clothesline. A pedlar came by and asked her in English, "How much do you want for the rug?" She, all bothered and not knowing how to tell him that the rug was not for sale, could not find another word to express herself but "nothing." The pedlar took the rug saying, "Thank you very much." It was to no avail that she ran after him shouting, "Nothing! Nothing!" The pedlar kept repeating,

"Thank you! Thank you!" and took her rug away.

After a few years of conducting their business in the summer, some pedlars decided to continue this form of trading year round. In the fall they would leave their merchandise with Dan (à Arsène) Doucet and with Lubin (à Baptiste) Aucoin. The local residents could then visit these homes and continue to barter.

In 1940, one of these pedlars, Harry Shore, opened a rug store in the home of Joe (à Theophile) Chiasson. He had bought many *breillon* rugs from the Chéticamp women, and he had also hired a few ladies—Mrs. Zabine (à Joe) Chiasson, Mrs. Marguerite-Marie (à Joseph à Den) and Mrs. Thérèse (à Charles à Émile) Beaudry—to hook woolen rugs for him, featuring a floral design. Each lady earned three dollars a week. He also hired Herbert LeBoutillier to advertise and sell these rugs to tourists who were increasing in number. In the summer, the rugs were exhibited outside, in front of the store, set up on frames on the lawn. This pretty sight attracted the tourists. However, the tourist season was short then and even if many rugs were sold and in spite of a ridiculously low labour cost, the business did not turn out to be profitable and the store was closed.

These pedlars, after a few years of profitable door-to-door selling, very often started their own stores in the urban centres of the province. One of them, who reportedly had earned $14,000 in a year selling rugs, opened a grocery store in New Waterford, Nova Scotia.

The era of the pedlars came to an end during World War II. It should be acknowledged that these pedlars were of service to the Chéticamp population by bringing and selling merchandise which could not be found in local stores at that time or by making it available at a slightly lower price. Chéticamp owes these pedlars recognition for having started the rug trade which from then on met with increasing success.

CHAPTER 5

Fledgling Beginnings, with Different Kinds of Rugs

When rugs were first hooked with wool by Chéticamp women, the patterns were ordered from John E. Garrett Ltd., New Glasgow, Nova Scotia. These pre-stamped jute canvases were called Bluenose patterns and usually featured a flower and a few leaves done in vivid tones.

Various materials

Wanting to economize, the women used a bit of everything to make rugs with jute canvas. They used woolen fabrics which they unravelled, carded, and spun again. They also used discarded cotton clothes which they cut in very narrow strips. They even used the starched red cotton wrapping of tobacco pouches. Because of its colour, this red cotton material was used to reproduce maple leaves of the fall season, the hearts which adorned the four corners of some rugs, as well as some flowers found in the centre of the rugs.

Jute was also used. The bags made of this material were carefully washed and then taken apart, strand by strand. These strands were then dyed in various colours. With the use of the spinning wheel, three of these strands were twisted together and knotted at both ends. During the process of hooking the rug, these knots were disposed of by cutting them under the canvas as soon as they were felt interfering with the hook. Spun and wound into a ball, jute was used in lieu of wool for making hooked rugs. The rugs made with jute were rougher than those made with wool, but they were beautiful nonetheless.

At Mick Boudreau's

Mick (à Antoine) Boudreau raised chickens, which meant that there were many jute sacks available since the chicken feed was supplied in such bags. Mick would save all the sacks. His wife Marie and their 16-year-old maid, Annie Roach, would wash the sacks, cut them up into tiny pieces, and churn them in order to turn them into *défaisures*. The resulting product was then spun and wound into balls. Prepared thus, it was an acceptable substitute for wool used in rug making.

[See colour photo 21.]

The process described above was long and arduous. Having thus processed many sacks, there were two left. Marie said to Annie, "Go and bury them under the manure pile where Mick will surely never find them, for if he saw them he would have us do as with the others, and I can't take any more."

This material, dyed in various colours, gave a fairly good finished product, beautiful rugs. One winter, Marie and Annie made a magnificent stairway rug covering each step. The background design consisted of different coloured squares emphasized by a black border on both sides.

Annie, who later became Mrs. Jimmy Larade, continued to make hooked rugs. Her most noteworthy contribution was an emblem, 24 feet square, with a red lion featured on a black background, the whole enclosed in red and yellow arabesques.

She and her daughter hooked many rugs, each ten square feet in area and featuring a big red lobster in the centre. In their first year in this venture, they sold ten of these rugs at the very lucrative price, for those days, of a dollar per square foot.

One hundred dollars in those days amounted to a small fortune!

At Moïse Aucoin's

Mrs. Malthide (à Moïse à Séverin) Aucoin and her daughters were the only ones to make *breillon* rugs which featured a particular design. Mrs. Maria Forest (à Napoleon) Fiset had given them the pattern. The rug consisted of coloured squares in ascending order. The particular difficulty with this pattern was to have a finished rug which featured squares of equal size and which matched in colour at each end on both sides. The Aucoins had discovered the solution to this problem; the rug had to be started in the centre.

Some women, among whom was Mrs. Marie Louise (à Tancrède) Chiasson, tried in vain to reproduce this pattern. Mrs. Chiasson's father-in-law, Den (à Lubin), had gone so far as to spend a whole evening, kneeling while taking various measurements with his folding foot-rule, trying to solve the puzzle [foot-rule: a measuring stick six feet long which can be folded to a length of six inches]. All his efforts were to no avail because he could not discover that the secret was to start in the centre. The next day, Mrs. Chiasson contacted the Aucoins who gave her the instructions on how to proceed successfully.

The Aucoins made many rugs featuring this pattern and, because they were especially beautiful, people would say, "Nobody can make beautiful *breillon* rugs like they do at Moïse à Séverin's."

The earlier days of rug making were characterized by considerable trial and error, as well as by excitement because the rugs were also beginning to sell well. Thus, wanting to make hooked rugs softer, Marguerite Gallant tried rolling the wool on her knees rather than spinning it in the traditional way. The result was a strand of wool which was less twisted and softer, but the wool thus "spun" was difficult to catch underneath the canvas with the hook. Even if the result was a softer rug, the difficulty of working with wool prepared this way made this procedure very unpopular.

At the MacFarlands'

It is a fact that many outside factors have contributed to the steady progressive movement towards the present perfection of hooked rugs made in Chéticamp. One person who contributed to this movement and who is worthy of mention was the wife of Joseph MacFarland, superintendent of the gypsum mine in Chéticamp.

The story of this family's life in Chéticamp as well as the type of rugs that were made in that household will be of interest to the reader and will give him a general picture of an important aspect of the social life in Chéticamp at that time.

The MacFarlands arrived from Boston (U.S.A.) in 1923 and stayed in Chéticamp until the closing of the gypsum mine in 1939.

Mrs. Agnes MacFarland was a woman of taste, an artist who devoted a lot of her time to fancy work: embroidery, knitting and sewing. She was also a good cook. She strived for perfection in everything she did. She also became interested in hooked rugs.

The MacFarlands lived successively in two large houses, first the one owned by Sandy (à William) Aucoin and then in the one owned by Robin Jones. They received many visitors, especially representatives of the gypsum mine. The MacFarlands needed the services of a maid, but Mrs. MacFarland was very demanding and in spite of the fact that they paid fifteen dollars per month, three dollars more than the prevalent wage, they had difficulty in finding one and more so in getting one to stay.

At the age of sixteen, Rose-Anna Chiasson, who was working for Charlie (à William) Aucoin for twelve dollars a month, decided that she wanted to earn more money. She offered her services to Mrs. MacFarland and the latter agreed to give her a week's trial. The eighth day over, the lady of the house told her, "You're the first maid who knows how to make my bed the way I like it. You're hired."

An account of Rose-Anna's work duties at the MacFarlands' is worth relating. It staggers the imagination; and all that was for fifteen dollars a month!

On Monday she would be up at 3:30 in the morning to light the stove and heat the water for the laundry. Electricity was not available in Chéticamp at that time. The family owned a clothes washer equipped with a mechanism which would stir the clothes when a handle was moved back and forth by hand. This was an improvement over the washboards with a wavy glass surface, which were used in all the other households. Nonetheless, Rose-Anna had to wash many sheets made from heavy cotton, many white tablecloths made with flax and which later had to be starched, fifteen white shirts, and the rest of the clothes. She also had to look after the household chores, polish the stove [with black-lead polish], sweep and dust everywhere.

Mr. MacFarland would get up at 7 o'clock. The maid prepared his breakfast, which included freshly cooked bran muffins because he insisted that they be baked daily. When he left for work, she went and opened the gate for him, similarly at night when he returned. Then she had to prepare breakfast for Mrs. MacFarland, who got up at 8 o'clock.

During the remainder of the week, Rose-Anna would get up at 5 o'clock. On Tuesday, using a gas iron, she would iron the clothes that she had washed the day before. She prepared the meals and, every day, also had to clean thirteen kerosene lamps. She washed the baby's bottles and prepared his milk. She bathed the dog. In summer, she even mowed the lawn.

She worked seven days a week until 11 at night, except for two nights when she was off. In spite of her incredible workload, Rose-Anna found the time to make rugs with Mrs. MacFarland. They would work at it especially at night. Friends of Mrs. MacFarland often came to help them with the hooked rugs. These friends were especially drawn by the beautiful patterns of these rugs. Rose-Anna dyed the wool; her mother, Mrs. Marie (à Charles à David) Chiasson would spin it, charging 25 cents a pound. Annie-Louise, Rose-Anna's sister, would stamp the patterns on the canvases.

As mentioned before, Mrs. MacFarland was an artist. She would strive hard to create new motifs and to have beautiful rugs made, especially for that era. A few are worthy of description.

For her bedroom, she had four rugs made. Two were ten square feet in area, one eight, and the fourth was shaped like a half-moon with an area of six square feet. The borders were done in a pale violet; the background was in the same colour but paler with multi-coloured flowers scattered throughout. For the children's room, three rugs featured flowers on a beige background with a dark pink border. For the halls, two rugs were made in a pale brown and featured dark brown plumes which bordered the whole rug, hooked in relief standing two inches higher than the background. Wool spun by the use of a spindle was used for the plumes. This wool was less twisted than the wool used for the remainder of the rug, hooked with wool which was spun in the usual fashion, using the spinning wheel. Once the ends of the woolen strands which made up the plumes were clipped, the latter looked like velours.

Even after Rose-Anna had left the MacFarlands to marry Amédée (à Arsène) Bourgeois, Mrs. MacFarland had further resort to her services and artistic talents. One year she brought Rose-Anna four beautiful white woolen blankets so that she could make a braided rug with them which was to be twelve by fourteen feet in area, that is 168 square feet. Rose-Anna dyed one blanket grey, another black, one pink and the last she dyed green. The blankets were then cut into strips and then braided, each colour of a different width.

These strands had to be sewn in spiral fashion and much skill was required so that the rug which was thus constructed would lay flat on the floor. Rose-Anna did an excellent job.

After Rose-Anna left her employ, Mrs. MacFarland hired several women to make her rugs. These women were paid 50 cents per day and worked from 8 in the morning until 5 at night. In those days money was scarce and those women were happy to have found work for which they were paid. They made several rugs for Mrs. MacFarland. An especially beautiful rug— one hundred square feet in area, featuring flowers and a medallion of roses in the centre on a black background highlighted by a pale blue border accentuated with yellow and golden spirals—is particularly memorable.

The MacFarlands' many visitors were amazed by all these rugs.

In 1939, the Mac-Farlands moved to Hali-fax and took occupancy of a large house which was rendered more lavish by their rugs.

Rose-Anna became a good friend of the MacFarlands and each time she went to Halifax she never failed to visit them. She made it her special duty to attend the funeral of Mrs. MacFar-land, who died at the age of 93.

The MacFarland

One of Mrs. MacFarland's tapestries on exhibition in the Élizabeth Lefort Gallery

children, who had preciously preserved all their mother's rugs, donated seven of them to La Société Saint-Pierre in 1982 so that they would be exhibited in the Élizabeth Lefort Gallery in Chéticamp.

These rugs, which are far from being as well finished as the rugs produced today and which will require retouching because of the wear which occured when they were in use, represent an important testimony and souvenir of the first years of this form of handcraft in Chéticamp.

Covers used in sleighs

The methods of making rugs were sometimes used to produce other necessary articles such as the covers used in *carrioles* [in Chéticamp, handsomely designed sleighs on elegant runners].

Up to 1930 and even later, automobiles were few in Chéticamp and they were used in the summer only because the roads were not plowed in the winter. During the cold season, people travelled in sleds or sleighs.

For protection against the cold, what was called sleigh pelts were used. The passengers in the sleighs wrapped themselves with these from their feet to their waists, sometimes right up to their necks. The more affluent people owned buffalo pelts; others used simple blankets. Other ladies with a more creative imagination had made more original covers to be used in the sleighs, adapting the methods of rug making to a different purpose. They used local cloth, woven and milled at home. Two-inch strips were cut from this cloth the lengths of which were indented with scissors. These strips were dyed in different colours and sewn one against the other on another piece of either blue or black cloth, according to the desired size. Because of their colours and the indentations in the fabric, these sleigh covers were simply magnificent.

Some sleigh covers were also made with a hook and wool or *défaisures* using jute canvas, but they were less flexible and less warm.

CHAPTER **6**

Important Turning Point in the History of Hooked Rugs: The Arrival of Miss Lillian Burke

The person who had an incomparable and dominating influence on Chéticamp's rug industry was Miss Lillian Burke, an important artist from New York.

    Miss Burke was endowed with a remarkable personality. Of optimistic inclination, she was vivacious and charming. She was also fortunate in her ability to be a leader, be it with groups of children or adults. Being a versatile artist, she could play the piano, paint, draw, model, sculpt and work with copper. Half Irish and half Polish, she seemed to have inherited the better character traits of these two nationalities *[see pages 147 to 149]*. Likeable, Catholic and able to speak some French, she had all that was necessary to be accepted at once by the ladies of Chéticamp.

Alexander Graham Bell's family

    How did it come to pass that Miss Burke became interested

in the hooked rugs produced in Chéticamp? Therein lies an interesting story which begins with the family of Alexander Graham Bell, the famous inventor of the telephone.

Mrs. Mabel Bell

Like several other celebrities, Alexander Graham Bell had chosen to build a summer home for his family in the charming countryside of Baddeck on Cape Breton Island. A remarkable humanitarian spirit was the driving force of this family. Mr. Bell's efforts to help the deaf are well documented. In this aspect, his wife did not take a back seat to him either. She devoted much of her time and energy to better the living conditions of her neighbours.

In 1894, she started five sewing schools for the young girls and ladies of Baddeck and its surroundings. The success she had with these courses encouraged her to start a project which she had been entertaining for some time. She had long thought about launching a particular form of handcrafts which would enable the ladies of the region to earn a bit of money.

Consequently, Mrs. Bell decided to teach these ladies the art of lacemaking. She bought the thread and cloth at wholesale price, supplied the patterns and directed the operation. She had intended the lace to be sold to the tourists who

Sample of Mrs. Bell's lace

35

visited the region during the summer months. Unfortunately, the tourists did not appreciate the work of the local ladies and preferred to buy commercial lace which was cheaper. This promising handcraft activity had to be discontinued.

When visiting New York in 1900, Mrs. Bell met Miss Burke who was, at the time, teaching fine arts in a Washington, D.C., school. Miss Burke immediately became a great friend of the Bell family which she visited often, in the years that followed, in Baddeck. In 1914 the Bell family invited her to come to Baddeck during the summer and teach the grandchildren the art of watercolour painting.

[See colour photo 2.]

Arrival of Miss Lillian Burke

After Mrs. Bell's death in 1922, her daughter, Mrs. Marian Fairchild, decided to revive the handcraft project which had been started by her mother. She then decided to invite her friend, the artist Lillian Burke, who liked Cape Breton very much, to direct the operation during the summer. Miss Burke gladly

Miss Lillian Burke

accepted the invitation and returned to Baddeck in the summer of 1924.

Mrs. Fairchild did not even begin to suspect that this invitation would eventually stimulate the hooked rug industry in Chéticamp and that her mother's original idea of organizing a profitable form of handcraft at the family level would, this time around, meet with extreme success.

Since the lacemaking venture had failed, Miss Burke chose another field of activity, namely hooked rugs. The ladies of

Baddeck had been making hooked rugs for a long time, sometimes with wool but more often with *breillons*.

Miss Burke supported this particular form of handcraft. In the hope of selling the rugs to the tourists, she herself would go around gathering the rugs, which she and Mrs. Fairchild would exhibit in the Gertrude Hall Library in Baddeck.

Their arrival in Chéticamp

It was understood that for her efforts, Miss Burke would keep ten percent of the sales. The first summer, her revenue was not considerable as the sale of the rugs totalled $1200. Her success was no better the following year. Miss Burke quickly realized that the lack of sales was due to the rough finish of the rugs, the colours used and the poor workmanship involved. She tried to bring improvements to these three aspects of the product, but the ladies of Baddeck resisted departing from their traditional patterns with their vivid colours. Faced with their reluctance to follow her advice, Miss Burke decided to look elsewhere and began to visit other regions of Cape Breton. Thus in 1927, she and Mrs. Fairchild arrived in Chéticamp.

Mrs. Marie-Jane Doucet, Miss Burke's agent

Because they did not speak French very well, and wanting some information, the ladies went to see Mr. Herbert LeBoutillier, the bilingual manager of the Robin Jones Store. Once he understood the purpose of their visit, he advised them to consult Mrs. Marie-Jane Doucet, restaurant owner, who was fairly conversant with the English language.

Miss Burke and Mrs. Fairchild explained to her the

Mrs. Marie-Jane Doucet

intent of their endeavour which they proposed to start in Chéticamp and invited her to act as intermediary between themselves and the ladies of the region.

Mrs. Doucet gladly accepted. She and her hostesses visited several women who were making rugs. Everywhere they visited, they were received cordially and warmly. Miss Burke quickly recognized the talent of the Chéticamp women in rug making and was quite happy to realize that they were receptive to her advice on how to improve their rugs and as ready to subscribe to her project.

The changing aspects of the rugs

Up to this point, the dye which came in envelopes, available in many colours and sold under the name of Diamond, was used to dye the wool. The local ladies used the colours as supplied, rarely mixed them to obtain different colours, and used vinegar as a fixing agent.

Miss Burke taught the ladies new techniques for dyeing wool. She also suggested that they use another form of dye called Irvin Dyestuff, manufactured in Germany, which she imported from the United States. As a fixative, she recommended the use of sulfuric acid instead of vinegar. She also taught them that with a proportionately balanced mixture of the primary colours, red, yellow and blue, they could obtain all the tints and nuances they wanted. She insisted that only pale and soft colours be used and recommended the use of wool of the first quality. The style of the rugs changed totally and this new look was the turning point which would eventually insure that this form of handcraft as produced in Chéticamp would become renowned.

Following these new directives, the ladies started to make small rugs, the patterns of which had been stamped by Miss Burke herself. Miss Burke, who lived in Baddeck during the summer, visited Chéticamp more frequently. During her absence, Mrs. Doucet coordinated the work of the ladies making rugs and made sure that the type of rugs produced were according to Miss Burke's directives. Mrs. Doucet would collect the rugs and forward them to Baddeck where Miss Burke and Mrs. Fairchild put them up for sale in their boutique. Mrs. Doucet was given ten percent of the sales.

It was understood that any rug which was not sold would be returned to its owner. The first year, the ladies fearing that they would lose their rugs in the shipping process, Mrs. Doucet could collect only seven rugs which she forwarded to Baddeck via the ship *Bras-d'or*. The tourists quickly bought these rugs and Mrs. Doucet received the proceeds which she distributed to those who had entrusted their rugs to her. That was the first time that anybody in Chéticamp was paid for making a rug. Consequently, the following year, Mrs. Doucet had no problem in finding two hundred rugs to send to Baddeck.

Every winter, Miss Burke would return to New York. However, the business of making rugs did not slow down because of her absence. In fact, it was during the winter that people had more free time to devote to rug making and it was during this season that more people were occupied by this activity, supervised by Mrs. Doucet.

Gradually, Miss Burke had larger rugs made and eventually some were produced that covered more than a hundred square feet. In the latter case, as many as ten women would gather in a home with enough room to accommodate a frame suitable for the dimensions of the rug, and there they would work on the rug for many weeks, even many months. In one case, a wall separating two rooms had to be knocked down in order to create the necessary space. Some houses had no room partitions upstairs; they were ideal for working on rugs of large dimensions. Later in the book, reference will be made to rugs which were set up and worked on in barns. Such was the case for the largest rug that Mrs. Doucet had produced under her supervision. It measured 400 square feet and required a frame which was much too big to be installed in a house.

This rug, which featured principally a floral design, required months of work by ten women. Once finished, the rug was very beautiful and was bought by an American amateur sailor.

In 1932, Marie-Jane Doucet, having been a widow for a few years, decided to take up residence with her children in Halifax. Her successor as intermediary for Miss Burke in Chéticamp was Mrs. Marie (à Willie à Hélène) Aucoin. Together with Miss Burke, Mrs. Doucet had in effect co-pioneered a new style of rugs and both had transformed the making of rugs into a financially rewarding business.

[See colour photo 4.]

That particular rug was hooked by Mrs. Marie-Jane Doucet and her daughter Agnès, using a much coarser wool than the one in current use. The colours found in this rug are the result of dyes obtained from onion peels and other vegetable matter. It was made before Miss Burke came to Chéticamp. The rug has always been in the possession of Mrs. Doucet's family, although it has been exhibited often across Canada. In the photograph, Agnès Doucet and her niece are holding the rug.

The dyes

Dyeing wool is a difficult operation at which some ladies excel, but which many others do not dare attempt. The first step is to start with very clean wool which is saturated with water. Water is brought to a boil in a vat or cauldron which is big enough that the wool will not be crowded in order to insure that the dyeing will be even throughout and not spotty.

Dye is poured into lightly boiling water and the mixture is stirred to make it uniform in colour. The wool is then soaked into the dye solution for a few minutes so that it will take on a bit of colour and then removed. The fixative is then poured into the dye solution and this mixture is stirred well to make it homogeneous. The wool is then boiled lightly in this mixture for twenty minutes; it is stirred constantly to ensure that it dyes uniformly. The wool is then removed from the solution and rinsed in lukewarm water. It is then spread out to dry.

Dyeing wool for a rug which requires one hundred different

colours or so is a still more delicate art. For each hue of colour desired, enough wool has to be dyed to suffice for the whole rug for it is very difficult to produce a tint which will match the original by dyeing a second time.

To obtain different shades or tints of a particular colour, the women would proceed thus: a skein of wool would be tied with a string at two or three intervals, or even more, according to the purposes of the person doing the dyeing. The skeins thus tied would be lowered into the dyeing solution up to the first string for a few minutes, then lowered to the second string for the same length of time and so on until the whole skein was soaked into the dye solution. This ingenious process created

Figure 9
A skein of wool tied with strings

tints or shades of one colour from dark to light as the part of the skein which was lowered first into the solution absorbed the dye during the entire process and the last part lowered absorbed the least dye. The result was a skein of wool which was of a dark colour at one end and diminished in colour intensity, giving a different shade or tint of the same colour at

Figure 10
A knotted skein of wool

the other end. It can easily be seen that to dye wool in multiple shades and tints for a rug requiring these varied hues was a tedious task for the ladies involved!

For dyeing the wool which would be used to hook the

From left to right:
Mrs. Luce Deveau, Mrs. Maggie Cormier and Mrs. Julienne Aucoin
at Point Cross River, gathered there to dye their wool

background of the rug, the women had discovered a more simple procedure. A skein of wool was knotted in the middle. The skein would then be soaked in the dyeing solution for twenty minutes. As the dye could not penetrate as easily the wool constituting the knot, they thus obtained a lighter shade of the colour for the remainder of the skein.

In the days when homes had no running water, the women, during the summer, would go to a river or brook to dye their wool. The necessary materials, that is the wool, the dye, the acid, the vats and the wood for building the fire, had to be transported to the chosen site. Everything was loaded into carts which the men drove to the brook or river in the morning and brought back home at night with the results of the day's work. So they would not waste time, the women would bring their spinning wheels and would spin the wool while the water heated up. When the water had reached the right temperature, they would dye their wool.

After, they hung the wool to dry on a nearby fence. At

certain places they even built a hearth (*foyer*) on which they could put a vat to heat the water.

Sulfuric acid

Any dye requires a fixative which will stop the colour from fading. Before Miss Burke came to Chéticamp, the ladies used vinegar for this purpose. Miss Burke recommended the use of the much more effective sulfuric acid. She obtained it for them and taught them how to use it.

Sulfuric acid is very strong; two ounces of it mixed in sixteen ounces of water makes a concentrated fixative. Two tablespoons of this solution is sufficient as a fixative for dyeing wool in a large vat.

The women who dyed the wool kept this solution in bottles which they made sure were out of reach of the children, because the acid is a deadly poison and can cause severe burns. No serious accidents, burns or poisoning were reported in Chéticamp, but there were several incidents involving this acid:

One woman had used too strong a concentration of sulfuric acid while dyeing her wool. With this wool, she hooked some flowers on canvas for a rug. The next morning she found her work on the floor. The acid had burnt through the canvas. The woman had to repair her canvas, wash the wool and redo the flowers.

Another woman had placed her bottle of fixative in the plate warmer of her stove. A drop of acid leaked from the bottle, ran down the length of a wall of the oven and burnt through the enamel down to the metal.

Mrs. Marie (à Charlie) Aucoin had left her bottle of acid on a window ledge in the sun. Unfortunately, the sun rays were very hot for the month of March. The bottle exploded and the acid sprayed the floor. How was she to clean this up? Sponging up the acid with rags was out of the question because she would have caused severe burns to her hands. Marie thought very fast and had an ingenious solution to her problem. She opened the door and shoveled snow on the floor, thus diluting the acid.

She then sprinkled a box of baking soda on the floor. She was then able to mop up the whole mess without burning her hands.

Mrs. Annie-Belle (à Eddie Joe) Aucoin feared thunderstorms. When it would thunder, like many others, she would take out a bottle of Holy Water and would sprinkle it in the form of a cross on the stove, the doors and the windows of the house. Once during a thunderstorm, after having "sprinkled" crosses around the house, she traced a cross on the baby's forehead much to the baby's discomfort. The baby began to cry. The following day there was a visible cross on her stove and her baby's forehead was all red. It was then that she realized that she had used acid rather than Holy Water.

Many ladies continued to use the dye produced by Dyestuff as well as sulfuric acid as a fixing agent long after the death of Miss Burke in 1952. A few, however, had always been faithful to the dye made by Diamond which offered a greater variety of colours, and throughout the years other ladies have reverted to the use of the dye produced by that manufacturer. However, Diamond dye is no longer available since 1960, and the dye used today is produced by Rit and Cushing which supplies almost every colour imaginable.

Because of the dangers involved with the use of sulfuric acid, most women have returned to the use of vinegar as a fixative. The usual proportion for the solution consists of one ounce of vinegar in the dye solution necessary to process four ounces of wool. A tablespoon of salt is also added.

CHAPTER 7

Miss Burke's Demands and Her Kindheartedness

The demands of Miss Burke

Mrs. Marie (à Willie à Helene) Aucoin, who succeeded Mrs. Marie-Jane Doucet as Miss Burke's intermediary, did so by virtue of her talents and her sense of organization. These qualities were indispensable at a time when the rug making industry was booming.

In New York, Miss Burke opened a studio and gallery where she displayed her rugs. She spent all of her time finding buyers, and stamping designs on the large rugs that they ordered. The stamping of the smaller rugs was left to Mrs. Aucoin. The canvases for the larger rugs, with the necessary colours indicated, were sent to Mrs. Aucoin who was responsible for having the rugs made by the local women. Mrs. Aucoin had to choose her workers, supervise the rug making, prepare for shipping and forward the finished product to New York.

Miss Burke would send some money with her orders so that the women could pay for the wool and dye. After she received the rugs, she sent the money which represented the salaries of the women who had worked on the rugs. Mrs. Aucoin apportioned the money to the women according to the number of hours or days they had worked on the project.

Miss Burke paid for the rugs by the square foot. Very often, when she ordered a large rug, she insisted on having a prototype of the rug made. This prototype was usually a square foot in size and featured all the colours which would be in the larger rug. These prototypes were sent to her so that she could evaluate the final result. Sometimes, she would require different prototypes with different shades of colour. Only when a prototype had been approved would the rug be started. Miss Burke did not pay for these prototypes; she paid for the actual rug only. These prototypes, which very often were very beautiful as well, were never returned to the people who made them.

Miss Burke was very demanding. In the summer when she came to Chéticamp, she visited her employees along with Mrs. Aucoin. She would have the finished rugs rolled out on

Prototype of a large rug

the floor and if a certain shade in the rug, which she herself had ordered, did not please her, she thought nothing of it to have that part of the rug unravelled and redone in another shade. She would stand on a chair to have a better vantage point to look at the rug and while pointing to a particular section of the rug would say, "A little more pinkish there" or "a little more yellowish here." After she had left, whenever timely, the employees would joke with a certain sarcasm, "A little more pinkish" or "yellowish here and there."

These alterations meant a lot of work. The large rug had to be remounted on the frame. The wool which did not please Mademoiselle because of its shade had to be removed, and new wool had to be dyed in the desired shade and worked into the rug again. Of course, Miss Burke paid for the work by the square foot once the rug had been finished to her satisfaction.

The designs of the large rugs always featured many flowers and leaves done in many different colours. Making these designs required long and tedious work. It happened that in a few households, in order to save work, a flower or a leaf was left out of the pattern, here or there, in the hope that Miss Burke would not notice. To no avail! She would spot the flaw immediately and insist that the pattern be redone to conform to the original. In this case, the ladies had nobody to blame but themselves.

After such experiences, it was not without a certain fear that the workers anticipated Miss Burke's visit to their home. One day, several people were working on a large rug in a local household. Everybody was edgy because they expected Miss Burke to visit them. While everybody was taking a work break, Léo (à Jean à Xavier) Roach jokingly hollered, "Here she does not come!" Having understood not what Léo had said but what they feared to hear, everybody pounced on the rug and began to work at great speed and in silence. Léo had a great laugh as he observed the panic which he had triggered.

Mrs. Rose (à Willie à Marcellin) Doucet, from the "Lac," was responsible for making a large rug. She had dyed the wool and hooked the rug with the help of other ladies. When the rug was finished and stretched out on the floor, she noticed that the background colour varied in shade giving a patchy effect. She took a chance and sent the rug to Miss Burke as such. All winter, however, she lived with the fear that Miss Burke would return the rug, as had already happened in Chéticamp.

At that time, there were no telephones in Chéticamp and news was transmitted by word of mouth on the church's steps on Sunday. People would gather on the steps ten minutes before mass for the purpose of learning all the news of the region. One Sunday, having returned from mass, Willie said to his wife, "I have very bad news for you. I really don't know how to begin." She answered, "I know. The rug has been returned!" "No," said he. "What then, if it is not the rug?" she replied. "Don't be afraid to tell me, for nothing could be worse!"

Unfortunately, it was more serious than she thought. Her father had died during the night.

A few weeks later, much to her great joy, she received the money for her rug.

Some of the women were more independent and were not as easily intimidated. Onésime Muise's wife, Élizabeth, was adept at stamping designs on rugs which varied from ten to twenty square feet in area. She performed this service for Marie LeLièvre's boutique and for Annie-Rose Chiasson. Mrs. Muise was also adept with the rug hook and could make some beautiful rugs. One day she had finished a rug of about twenty square feet in area for Miss Burke. The main design of the rug was the helm of a ship against a blue-grey background, overall a pleasant effect. Miss Burke found that the blue-grey background was not uniform in shade and wanted to unravel the offending sections herself. Said Élizabeth, "If you undo it, you'll finish it yourself. Some women are scared of you, but I'm not one of them." Miss Burke left the rug alone and bought it as it was.

In spite of her developed artistic taste, it happened that Miss Burke made mistakes in her evaluation of some rugs. She had a pattern of a Persian horse of which she used to have several copies made. Only three colours, brown, beige and gold, were to be used. Around 1938 Mrs. Catherine (à William) Larade, who had agreed to hook one of these rugs, decided— without consulting Miss Burke—to change the colours and to use red, black and white. The following spring when Miss Burke came for the rug, she was disappointed and refused to buy it. However, the following autumn, Mrs. Marie (à Willie) Aucoin shipped it to an exhibition in Toronto along with several other rugs. The rug caught the eye of Lady Tweedsmuir, wife of the Governor General of Canada, who bought it as a Christmas gift for her son. Mrs. Larade would never have dreamed to be so honoured as to have one of her rugs adorn the walls of Rideau Hall.

[See colour photo 5.]

Since then the Persian horse design is reproduced in Chéticamp with the colours used by Mrs. Larade and is a popular selling rug.[1]

While it is true that Miss Burke was very demanding and sometimes harsh with her employees, it is also true that, by her intransigence, she instilled in them a sense of the perfect and an artistic taste which today are the main characteristics of rugs made in Chéticamp.

Lillian Burke's kindheartedness

Even if Miss Burke was demanding, it must not be said that she was not kindhearted. To the contrary, she was very glad of the economic help which the rug business was bringing to the families in those days of poverty. When visiting Chéticamp with Mrs. Fairchild, she would remark happily, here and there, "Look at that newly painted house, that sizeable addition, that new roof. Well! All that is thanks to the money earned by making rugs."[2]

Whichever homes she visited, she always had gifts, candies, toys, etc., for the children. Also she never forgot to send small gifts to her employees at Christmas time. The women whom she felt more meritorious, those who showed great industry in spite of a handicap, be it a sore back or some other physical

One of Miss Lillian Burke's parties at Willie (à Hélène) Aucoin's

These feasts always ended with a dance [photos by Gilbert Grosvenor
obtained from the National Geographic Society, 1940]

ailment, were particularly remembered at that time of year.

Miss Burke had a happy personality; she had the soul of a poet and liked beautiful things. In autumn, when she travelled from Baddeck to Chéticamp, she would fill her pockets with lupine seeds which she had gathered in the Bell family garden, and these she sowed along the road so that when they would grow, the flowers would embellish the countryside.

Each summer, she would organize a family picnic for her many employees and their children. This village festival would take place on the threshing-floor of the barn of her agent, Mrs. Marie (à Willie) Aucoin. The festival would start at the beginning of the afternoon. Miss Burke directed the activities, which usually started with party games. Games such as "Who's got the button?"[3], musical chairs[4], rope jumping, foot races, potato sack races, etc., were popular. Each winner would receive a small reward. The games were followed by a square dance to the music of Joseph (à Athanase) Larade's fiddle.

Following the dance, Miss Burke would serve a delicious lunch featuring cakes, cookies and soft drinks. These little treats were bought at local stores and did not cost much, but in 1933 when most people in Chéticamp could not afford as much, they were in effect a luxury.

One summer, Miss Burke extended her graciousness to inviting Chéticamp ladies to spend an afternoon with her in Baddeck. Fifteen accepted the invitation and travelled to Baddeck seated on benches in the back of Léo (à William) Cormier's truck. Miss Burke lived with the Bells in a house the beauty of which had never been seen by these Chéticamp ladies. The spacious grounds with their beautiful green lawns, the long stately flower beds in bloom, and the stately trees gave our ladies the feeling that they were in heaven. Miss Burke greeted them warmly, had them visit the property, and ended the reception with a lunch served under the trees on lawn tables. The lunch consisted of sandwiches, cookies and cakes accompanied by tea brewed from tea bags. The ladies were totally dumbfounded to discover a tea bag in each of their cups, with a little string with a piece of paper attached to each string hanging over the cup's rim, so that the tea bag could be removed from the cup once the tea had steeped. The ladies had never experienced the like! They were of the consensus that one had to be a millionaire to be able to afford such luxury!

The ladies returned from Baddeck filled with as much wonder as the first astronauts who returned from the moon. A few days later one of them, Mrs. Judith (à Polite à Gabriel) Boudreau, described her trip to a friend. The latter exclaimed: "The world is a big place, isn't it!" "Yes," answered Mrs. Boudreau, "you can certainly say that again!"

For most of these ladies who had never ventured out of Chéticamp, travelling to Baddeck (65 kilometres) amounted to going to the end of the world!

1. See also colour photo 41: another large rug for Rideau Hall. In 1998, Marie-Claire Doucet and a team of "hookers" successfully completed a rug of gigantic proportions for one of the rooms in Rideau Hall, home to Canada's Governor General, in Ottawa. Marie-Claire was helped by Lucy Larade, Hilda Poirier, Sylvia Roach, Irene Fraser and Brenda Doucet.

The rug pays homage to Canada's provincial flowers as they are its focal point. Marie Elmwood of the Maritime Museum in Halifax came up with this concept, and Gilles Deveau of Chéticamp, draftsman by trade, stamped the design on the canvas. To accommodate a canvas of such large dimensions, a special frame was needed, and Clarence LeLièvre was hired to build one. It was Marie-Claire who had the responsibility of dyeing and preparing the wool. The task at hand meant that she had to dye 72 skeins of wool for the background alone, 48 more skeins of green shades for the leaves, and numerous other colours for the floral design.

Although it is far from the largest rug ever hooked in Chéticamp, it necessitated approximately four million stitches and 82 pounds of wool! The tapestry measures 10 $^{1}/_{2}$ feet by 15 feet.

2. Marion H. Bell Fairchild, "Cape Breton's Debt to Lillian Burke," *Handcrafts*, Department of Trade and Industry, Halifax, N.S., October 1952.

3. See *Chéticamp: History and Acadian Traditions*, by Father Anselme Chiasson. Breton Books, Wreck Cove, N.S., 1998, p. 174.

4. *Ibid.* "Jeux d'élimination (Elimination Games)," p. 185.

CHAPTER 8

The Extraordinary Development of the Rug Making Industry

In a rather short time, Miss Burke was successful in starting in Chéticamp a genuine rug making business. She started by selling the rugs to tourists in Baddeck, but she soon opened up other markets particularly in New York. From New York, where she would spend the winters, she sent the orders as well as the designs for the rugs to her agent, Mrs. Marie (à Willie) Aucoin. Mrs. Aucoin would see to it that the work was done, including the one-square-foot prototypes which Miss Burke always demanded to see before the rugs were made.

In the spring, she would arrive with many new orders and different patterns.

Miss Burke's artistic talents served her well when it came to designing beautiful patterns which she stamped on the canvas herself. These artistic designs made famous the Chéticamp rugs and the people who crafted them.

This business developed during the economic depression which lasted until World War II. Money was scarce in Chéticamp. The rug industry was proving to be a real unexpected windfall. The village became a veritable "rug making workshop." Men as well as women, young men and young ladies, whole families—almost everybody was involved with rug making.

Unfortunately, it is impossible to mention all the families which were involved in this activity. It will be interesting, however, to focus on some families and on certain persons in particular, to give an account of the difficulties encountered with the production, especially of the large rugs. We will also focus on the social activity which accompanied rug making, on some of the magnificent works completed and, often, on the illustrious people who acquired them.

Mrs. Luce (à Charlie à Polite) Deveau

Mrs. Luce (à Charlie à Polite) Deveau was one of the women who could make some of the most beautiful *breillon* rugs. She would adorn them with hearts, flowers and coloured leaves. For the material of the hearts, flowers and leaves she used fabrics of the desired colour such as the one used to wrap tobacco pouches, for example, or she dyed white fabrics the colour she wanted.

After the arrival of Miss Burke, Mrs. Deveau converted her rug making to woolen rugs. Her home became a permanent workshop where the larger rugs, four hundred and even five hundred square feet, were produced one after the other. A large frame for hooking these rugs was a permanent cumbersome fixture of her home. One of these frames was so large that in order to be able to walk completely around it, a partition of the pantry had to be knocked down. This frame required five rollers, each ten feet in length, one of them being the bottom roller with its rack and pinion. That particular frame had been made by Mr. Deveau using his axe as his only tool.

One year, Miss Burke had ordered three large rugs of the same pattern featuring flowers, leaves and bows of ribbons as motifs. She had specified all the colours she wanted except for the bows, the colour of which she was not able to decide. The three rugs were made accordingly and the space which represented the bows of ribbon was left untouched; the rugs were unmounted from the frame in turn while Miss Burke's arrival was awaited. When she arrived in the spring and she saw the overall effect of the rug, she was able to decide which subdued colour she wanted for the ribbons. In order that the ten women who had worked on the three rugs be given work, as they could not all work on the ribbon designs of the one rug, the three rugs were mounted in the same house, one in the kitchen-living room, one in the dining room and the third in a bedroom. [The first floor of an Acadian house usually consisted of a bedroom, a dining-room and another large room bigger than the others where the people spent most of their time and where the food was cooked on a stove. In fact, this room was a sort of a kitchen and living-room combined.]

The ladies, neighbours and friends, worked continually at making rugs with Mrs. Deveau. Before the rug could be started, it was necessary to prepare the wool. They would meet in a particular place, each with her spinning wheel, to spin in one day the necessary wool. This gathering was called a *filerie*. The supper, which featured a pudding or a *fricot*, finished off the spinning bee. [In Acadia, the morning meal is called "breakfast," the noon meal "dinner," and the evening meal "supper."]

After the wool was spun, it was dyed in various colours. During the winter, the dyeing of the wool was done in the home; during the summer, it was done at Point Cross River.

When a large rug was finished, naturally, many small pieces of wool of all the colours used were left over. Not wanting to waste anything, the ladies were happy when Miss Burke would order a rug with small multi-coloured motifs, such as birds for example. These motifs would enable the women to use the small pieces of leftover wool and would save them the arduous chore of dyeing some more.

When about ten women gathered in one house to work on a large rug, not to mention the visitors who were attracted as well by this activity, it was inevitable that some funny and amusing things would happen.

Miss Burke wanted a 450-square-foot rug made, for which she had specified that she wanted a dirty-grey background. Four prototypes of the rug had been sent to her and each time Miss Burke had found the background colour to be insufficiently "dirty." In those days Mr. Deveau, like all the men of Chéticamp, wore woolen pants, the material for which was woven on the loom, fulled [likely shrunk and thickened by pounding on a table at a milling frolic], and dyed a very dark grey. Mrs. Deveau discovered a solution to her problem after she had finished washing her husband's pants. Mrs. Deveau realized that when she rinsed the pants, their colour would run and the rinse water was really a dark dirty grey. Having a sudden bright idea, she said, "I guarantee you that Miss Burke will find the fifth prototype dirty enough!" She immersed skeins of wool in the rinse water and let them soak for a long time. Miss Burke's answer came back saying that the prototype, this time, was perfect. The rug was therefore made using for background material the wool which had been dyed in the rinse water of Mr. Deveau's pants.

The women would work on the rugs until 9 o'clock at night. As there was no electricity in Chéticamp yet, they used kerosene oil lamps as their source of light. The lamps were placed as close as possible to the women working on the rug. Often the older ladies would admonish the mischievous younger ones, saying, "Be very careful not to upset that lamp!"

A tin can filled with kerosene was always kept in a corner of the room. As was customary, each night before finishing work, Mrs. Maggie (à Léo à William) Cormier would recite the rosary and the others would participate in the prayer. Mrs. Cormier, however, had trouble counting the beads between the *Pater Nosters* [Our Fathers] while continuing her work on the rug. One night she asked a young man to give her a signal when it would be time for the next *Pater Noster*. The next *Pater Noster* coming up, the young man hit the tin can with a metal bar. At the resulting noise, everybody jumped up and cried out in surprise and then broke out in laughter. The reciting of the rosary ended then and there.

PHOTO 1: This tapestry, "The Crucifixion," was made by Élizabeth Lefort in 1964 and has an area of 55 square feet. It is exhibited at Les Trois Pignons.

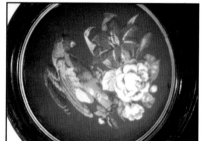

Photo 2: Miss Lillian Burke, a New York artist, is recognized as the founder of the hooked rug industry in Chéticamp.

Photo 3: One of Mrs. Maria Forest Fiset's rugs which was made in the 1870s.

Photo 4: A rug made before the arrival of Miss Burke to Chéticamp in 1927, by the late Mrs. Marie-Jane Doucet and her daughter Agnès (standing at left in this photograph). It is a rare sample of this kind of early work.

Photo 5: This "Persian Horse" is a reproduction of a rug which was bought by Lady Tweedsmuir in 1938 and which was displayed in Rideau Hall in Ottawa.

Photo 6: "The Tree of Life" was presented to Queen Elizabeth II in 1976 when she visited Nova Scotia. It was made by Marie and Joseph-Léo Muise. A reproduction of this rug is exhibited in the Élizabeth Lefort Gallery.

Photo 7: This rug, hooked by Mrs. Catherine Poirier, is part of the collection owned by Mrs. Dorothy Harley Eber and Mrs. Jane Mackeen Fagan.

PHOTO 8: A rug made by Miss Antoinette Deveau and Mrs. Nanette Aucoin.

PHOTO 9: This winter scene was produced by Mrs. Flora Deveau and was given to one of her sisters in the United States. The rug is now at the home of Mrs. Georgie (Armelle) Aucoin, daughter of Mrs. Flora Deveau.

PHOTO 10: "A French Kitchen" hooked by Annie-Rose and Gérard Deveau.

PHOTO 11: A rug depicting the "Dispersion of the Acadians" which is exhibited at the "Centre de la survivance acadienne" in Memramcook. It was made by Mrs. Sadie Roach, Mrs. Ethel Deveau, Mrs. Marie-Adèle Poirier and Mrs. Marie-Louise Cormier.

PHOTO 12: A scene of Peggy's Cove which was hooked by Sadie and Paulite Roach and presented to Prince Charles and Princess Diana on the occasion of their visit to Nova Scotia in 1983.

PHOTOS 13, 14 AND 15: Besides floral designs, the women of Chéticamp also know how to make logoes and emblems which very often are difficult to reproduce because of the colours and letters.

PHOTO 16: The Honourable Pierre Elliot Trudeau is presented with a rug by Miss Louise Aucoin in commemoration of his visit to Chéticamp in 1971.

PHOTO 17: Mrs. Marie-Louise Cormier is particularly talented when it comes to dyeing wool. Many hours of meticulous work are sometimes required to produce the desired shades of colour.

PHOTO 18: This rug was made in 1940 by parishioners for Saint Peter's Church following a request by Father LeBlanc. A part of this rug, which measured 75 square feet, is now in Father Fiset's tomb in the basement of Saint Peter's Church.

PHOTO 19: This rug was made in 1981 and was presented to the Acadian Federation of Nova Scotia. From left to right: Annie-Rose Deveau, Annie Roach, Thérèse Chiasson, Evelyne Aucoin, Marie-Rose Deveau, Thérèse Aucoin, Henriette Aucoin, Laurette Larade and Gérard Deveau.

PHOTO 20: A rug having an area of 63 square feet (7 x 9 feet) was made by Mrs. Joseph à T. C. LeBlanc.

PHOTO 41: Opposite, a portion of the large rug at Rideau Hall, Ottawa, made in 1998. From the top, clockwise, the floral emblems of the provinces of Canada: Lady's Slipper of Prince Edward Island, Fireweed of the Yukon, Mountain Avens of the Northwest Territories, Mayflower of Nova Scotia, Purple Violet of New Brunswick, Wild Rose of Alberta, Pitcher Plant of Newfoundland and Labrador, Pacific Dogwood of British Columbia, Prairie Crocus of Manitoba, White Trillium of Ontario, Western Red Lily of Saskatchewan; at the centre, Fleur-de-Lis of Québec.

PHOTO 21: When the rug making industry first started, the Chéticamp women often had to be ingenious. Nothing was wasted. These photographs show a group of women in the process of recycling old stockings to recover from them wool which would be suitable for hooking rugs.

PHOTO 41

PHOTO 22: "La Sagouine," based on a description from Antonine Maillet's book by the same title, was hooked by Mrs. Henriette Aucoin. The rug is exhibited in the Élizabeth Lefort Gallery.

PHOTO 23: "The Bluenose," made by Sadie and Paulite Roach, is exhibited in the Élizabeth Lefort Gallery.

PHOTO 24: A view of Chéticamp as seen from Chéticamp Island made by Mrs. Adèle Poirier on a canvas stamped by Dominique Maillet.

PHOTO 25: This rug was presented to Father Charles Aucoin (standing to the right) by La Sociétè Saint-Pierre in recognition of his research into the genealogical backgrounds of Chéticamp families. The rug was made by Mr. and Mrs. Gérard Deveau and is exhibited in the Élizabeth Lefort Gallery.

PHOTO 26: This rug represents the life history of Mr. John Mudge from Connecticut (standing at right). The rug has an area of 24 square feet (4 x 6 feet) and was designed and hooked by Mr. and Mrs. Gérard Deveau.

PHOTO 27: "Cap Rouge Rock" made by Mrs. Antoinette Lefort. It is exhibited in the Élizabeth Lefort Gallery.

PHOTO 28: This representation of a seagull, hooked by Miss Marie-Edna Roach, is exhibited in the Élizabeth Lefort Gallery.

PHOTO 29: This rug featuring birds was hooked by Mrs. Antoinette Lefort who is renowned for working with this kind of motifs.

PHOTOS 30 AND 31: Courses in rug making are available to the people of the region, teaching them how to improve their technique or teaching them the art of rug making. The courses are taught at Les Trois Pignons.

PHOTO 40: Diane Poirier, manager of the Coopérative artisanale.

Photo 32: "The Spirit of Flight" was made in Chéticamp in 1930 for Mr. Casey Baldwin to commemorate the first airplane flight in Canada. This flight took place in Baddeck, Nova Scotia, on February 23, 1909.

Photo 33: The character "Giant Lady of the Night" was taken from the story "Tit-Jean Quatorze," from Antonine Maillet's book, *Pélagie-la-charrette* . This tapestry was hooked in 1982.

PHOTO 34, 35 AND 36: Photographs taken inside various rug and tapestry boutiques showing the beauty as well as the remarkable variety of rugs.

PHOTOS 37: "Jesus the Adolescent" covers an area of 12 square feet and features 370 colours. It was made in 1963.

PHOTO 38: "The Nativity" features 71 colours and was made in 1962. It covers an area of 11 square feet.

PHOTO 39: This scene was produced in 1967 and represents Canada's Centennial. It features 416 colours, 1,750,000 stitches (loops), and covers an area of 66 square feet.

These three tapestries were made by Élizabeth Lefort and are exhibited in the gallery which bears her name at Les Trois Pignons.

In the summertime, Miss Burke would not fail to visit her employees. Very often, she would be accompanied by Mrs. Marian Fairchild, Alexander Graham Bell's daughter, by Mrs. Fairchild's children, and sometimes by her nieces. All these people, who were really all very likeable, would inspect the rugs with Miss Burke. The employees resented this somewhat and would refer to the others as "the meddlesome biddies of Baddeck."

If the visit of the ladies took place in the afternoon, it was customary to serve them a lunch after they had examined the rugs thoroughly. The economic conditions had improved somewhat in 1938 and 1939 and so had the lunches, which usually consisted of cake, cookies and tea but no sandwiches as Miss Burke did not eat bread. On one occasion, as she was preparing the lunch while Mrs. Cormier was chatting with the guests, Mrs. Deveau realized that no cake nor cookies were available. She prepared sandwiches for the others and ran over to Mrs. Cormier's to fetch some cake for Miss Burke. The latter accepted a second cup of tea, but Mrs. Deveau did not have a second piece of cake to offer her. Mrs. Cormier had noticed this and after the guests had departed she said to Mrs. Deveau, "So, you had no cake left and to think that I had a similar cake at home!" Because they were neighbours she added, "You could have gone over to my place to get some." Mrs. Deveau answered, "It's your cake I served, but I didn't bring enough!" The preceding anecdote gives an idea of the friendliness of the neighbourhood and how these women would help one another.

In the years 1938-1939, Miss Burke paid 75 or 80 cents per square foot of rug—that is, when the rug had actually reached New York and had received her approval. Even then it could be six months to a year before the women got paid for their work. Meanwhile the ladies who would not receive news from New York would entertain doubts and worry that the rugs had been lost on the way to New York or were being returned by Miss Burke. Naturally they were very happy when finally their money arrived.

Mrs. Annie (à Joseph à Jean) Chiasson (1902-1972)

Mrs. Annie (à Joseph à Jean) Chiasson made several large rugs for Miss Burke. She even had the honour of being asked to make the largest rug which was ever produced in Chéticamp.

It is said that this rug was a replica of one in the Louvre in Paris. Miss Burke spent three months stamping the design on the canvas. The rug used 200 pounds of wool which Mrs. Chiasson—starting with the primary colours red, yellow and blue—had to dye into 120 different colours as required by the design.

Not having any running water in her home, Mrs. Chiasson transported the wool, the dye, the acid, the vats and a small wood-burning stove to a brook near "la source Bouillante" and there, in a swamp, she dyed all the wool.

The rug measured 18 by 36 feet, that is, 648 square feet in area. The frame needed to mount the canvas for a rug this size required much more space than was available in the homes. This frame also was set up in the threshing area of a barn. Under the supervision of Mrs. Marie (à Willie) Aucoin, Miss Burke's agent, nine people worked six months to produce the rug: Mrs. Annie Chiasson, Mrs. Emma Haché, Miss Élizabeth Haché, Mrs. Esther Boudreau, Miss Edna Boudreau, Miss Luce-Yvonne Aucoin, Miss Philomène Bourgeois, Miss Luce

A few of the women who worked on this large rug of 648 square feet in area: From left to right, Mrs. Emma Haché, Mrs. Annie Chiasson, Miss Luce Bourgeois, Miss Philomène Bourgeois, Mrs. Esther Boudreau, Miss Marie Aucoin, Miss Élizabeth Haché and Miss Alice Aucoin. The little girl on the rug is Thérèse Chiasson, daughter of Mrs. Annie Chiasson.

This magnificent 648-square-foot rug (36' x 18')
is somewhere in Virginia

Bourgeois and Miss Marie Aucoin. The ladies worked every day of the week from 8 in the morning until noon and from 1 in the afternoon until 5 and finally from 6 to 9 o'clock at night. They would take only a ten-minute break in the morning and the afternoon to relax a bit and eat their own individual lunches of bread and butter.

To produce such a large rug, the frame had to have five rollers to wind up the completed part as it was finished. The rollers became very big and consequently very heavy to turn. To produce such a rug was very tiring, but the people of Chéticamp were very proud of having produced such a masterly and magnificent rug. This rug is now somewhere in Virginia. In spite of extensive research, it was impossible to find the location and the owner of this rug.

On another occasion, these same ladies had made a rug which was almost as big; but when it was finished, Miss Burke was not ready to buy it. Naturally, many rumours flew, producing much anxiety: "She has gone bankrupt! Customs officers have arrested her, etc." This rug of hundreds of square feet had to be kept in the home of Joseph Chiasson, rolled on the floor in a corner of a room for three months, before it was finally shipped to Miss Burke.

Mrs. Chiasson was responsible for the rugs which were produced in her home. One summer's day when Miss Burke was visiting, she disapproved of a section of a large rug which she wanted done again. A young man, Stanislaus Gaudet, who was also working on the rug, took a picture of Miss Burke while she was expressing her dissatisfaction to Mrs. Chiasson. Miss Burke was shocked by this and had her agent tell him that he was not to work on the rugs anymore. However, as nobody could be found to replace him, he was kept on.

So many people working together all day long for months made for intense group interaction which had its share of joking and teasing. As stated before, each woman would always bring her own bread and butter for the lunch breaks in the morning and in the afternoon. As the saying went, if a woman was to eat the crusty end of the loaf of bread, which was called "the ass end," she would marry a widower. Evidently, whenever a single girl bit into the crusty end of the loaf she would be teased, "Watch it, or you'll marry a widower!" Luce Aucoin who had married a widower heard on many an occasion, "You must have eaten the 'ass' of many loaves before you nabbed your widower!"

At Joseph Chiasson's, the minute that the ladies started working on the rug in the morning, they would sing some of the chants associated with the mass such as the Kyrie, the Gloria, the Sanctus, etc. Joseph who had been tending to the livestock in the barn would arrive a bit later and tiptoe to the stairs, and sitting on the step would say, "I'm late for mass again!"

All these ladies have continued hooking rugs even after Miss Burke was not interested anymore. Especially remembered are the small tapestries, two square feet in area, featuring young shepherds, which required many shades of wool. These beautiful tapestries which required a lot of work were sold for eight dollars each or, as was often stated ironically by the ladies, "the price of a young piglet." In fact, every spring, the Scots from neighbouring villages would arrive with piglets which they sold for eight dollars each.

A sense of humour was obviously current in these groups and helped to make the fatigue of long days of work bearable.

Another case in point: Mrs. Clara (à Willie à Polite) Bourgeois would work constantly on large rugs. However, she worked with difficulty because of chronic backache. To ease her suffering she continually wore a plaster between her shoulders. In Chéticamp they call this plaster a *sirouane*. Having worked on a large rug from June 25th to October 27th, she exclaimed, "This is much too strenuous for my *sirouane!*"

The stories associated with certain rugs are at times touching. In 1940, several ladies hooked a 125-square-foot rug for Mrs. René Boucher, wife of the manager of the Royal Bank of Canada in Chéticamp. Mrs. Boucher was very proud of the rug which graced the floor of her living room. The Bouchers lived in Chéticamp for several years before moving to Bouctouche, New Brunswick. In 1980, their son Billy came back to Chéticamp with the rug which had been bequeathed to him by his mother at her death. The rug had been in use for forty years and consequently was damaged in a few places. Mr. Gérard Deveau and Mrs. Marie-Rose (à Paul) Deveau took on the task of repairing the rug in the workshop at Les Trois Pignons. One year later, when Billy returned to pick up his rug, he couldn't believe how successful the restoration had been. The rug, which was like new, was the best souvenir his mother had left him.

Another case is interesting. Around 1950, some Chéticamp ladies had made a 60-square-foot rug featuring a floral design on a beige background with a deep pink border. The rug was bought for Princess Elizabeth, later Queen Elizabeth II, as a gift from the province of Nova Scotia to commemorate her first visit to Canada. At that time, a piece of canvas big enough to make such a large rug was not available in Chéticamp. As a solution to this problem, two pieces of canvas were sewn together. Because of the resulting seam, which was visible on the bottom side only, the organizing committee for the visit decided not to present the rug to the Princess.

Much later, in 1983, some women from Chéticamp were present in Sydney for a three-day promotion program organized by the Mayflower Mall. On exhibition were rugs made in Chéticamp, and Mrs. Henriette (à Eddie) Aucoin was present to give demonstrations on how to hook a rug.

As it happened, Mr. and Mrs. Allen Sutherland, formerly from Vancouver but now residing in Halifax, had travelled to Cape Breton around that time and visited the exhibition. An aunt of this couple had bought the rug which was originally to be presented to Princess Elizabeth and had given it to them as a gift. Having embellished the living room floor for more than thirty years, the rug was damaged. Not knowing how to go about having it repaired, they had been transporting it with them in their automobile for several months. They knew that the rug had been meant as a gift for Princess Elizabeth and that, to them, made the rug more valuable. Needless to say, they were very happy to meet Mrs. Henriette Aucoin and have her restore the rug, which was returned to them as good as new.

Original design of a rug made at Joseph (à Jean) Chiasson's

This four-by-six-foot rug had been made by a few women at the home of Mrs. Annie (à Joseph) Chiasson. They had no pre-stamped design for it, so they created their own and decided on the appropriate tints of wool for the rug. As for the cat which was featured in the rug, the model for it was Mrs. Chiasson's own cat which "posed" on the table while she (the cat) was drawn on canvas. While the women worked on the design of the cat and were trying to faithfully reproduce the nuances of colour of the cat's fur, the cat was stretched out on the canvas where she remained immobile while being petted. Once the rug was finished, it was very beautiful and the cat looked almost lifelike.

At Placide (à Lubin) Boudreau's

One could always find a large rug mounted on a frame at Placide Boudreau's home. Throughout the years of rug making at her home, Luce, Placide's wife, dyed the wool. The motifs were stamped on canvas first by Miss Burke, then by Mrs. Marie (à Willie) Aucoin and finally by Mrs. Marie (à Charlie à Lubin) Aucoin, depending on who was supervising the work. Several people were working on these large rugs, among them a neighbour Mrs. Olive (à Joseph à Fabien) Deveau and several teenaged boys and girls, whom Mrs. Boudreau and Mrs. Deveau watched closely. The young people were mischievous and were prone to waste their time playing. Mrs. Boudreau would glance over the top of her eyeglasses and say to them, "Hookez, hookez! pour rouler!" [Translator's note: A literal translation of this sentence is not possible. In effect, it was Mrs. Boudreau's way of telling the young people that the faster they would work, the sooner the rug would be completed.]

The people worked at these rugs every day and every night of the week except Sunday. However, if on a particular night a dance was scheduled in the district, Mrs. Boudreau or Mrs. Deveau would designate a sizeable section of the rug for the young people to work on and would say to them, "If you finish that before supper, you will not have to work tonight." In effect, the young people had been told that they could go to the dance. The ladies were sure that the work would be completed before suppertime.

Each night, the day's work was ended, without fail, with the reciting of the rosary. One night, however, Zabeth Muise left before the rosary was recited because her friend and future husband, Simi-John Deveau, was waiting for her outside the house to take her to a dance. The next morning she was reprimanded in such a way that she never dared leave early again.

Mrs. Marie (à Joseph à Victor) Roach (1887-1958)

Mrs. Marie (à Joseph à Victor) Roach always had large rugs mounted at home, on which her three daughters—Marie-Louise, Marie-Cézaire and Marie-Edna—would work, as well as five or six other women—Claire and Emma Haché, Mrs. Esther Boudreau and her daughter Edna, Laurette Boudreau and Annie Deveau. Mrs. Roach processed all of the wool and her daughter Marie-Louise dyed it.

The largest of the rugs she produced required a frame which went from one corner to the other across the living room. This room was rendered non-functional for several months while the rug was being made.

Work on the rugs would begin at 8 o'clock in the morning and would continue into the evening. Spending such long days doing nothing but handling a hook could have been very monotonous, but Mrs. Roach owned a battery radio and at 8 o'clock sharp the radio would be tuned to New Carlisle (Québec) for a religious program hosted by Father Lionel Boisseau. During Lent, the women who worked on the rug sang the mass in Latin. During the month of March, they recited a long prayer in honor of Saint Joseph. In May and October, the months devoted to the Virgin Mary, the women recited the rosary.

During the day other radio programs were tuned in, such as "Grande soeur" in the morning, "Rue principale" in the afternoon and "Un homme et son péché" in the evening. These serials and other programs were listened to religiously, in silence, while the women worked.

The rest of the time, between radio programs and prayer, was usually animated by conversation and teasing. Practical jokes were also played at times.

Elie Roach, Joseph's brother, liked to play the following practical joke: the women would always wear an apron, and Elie would untie the strings in the back and tie them to a crossbar of their chairs. They would only notice the prank when they would attempt to leave their chairs and drag them along with them. Unfailingly, the result of this prank was cries, fake threats and laughter.

Marie-Edna Roach (1924-   )

Marie-Edna Roach, daughter of Mrs. Marie Roach, is worthy of special mention. Having worked on rugs with her mother since she was young, she went on to make her own mark in this field of handcrafts. She hooked rugs, first for Miss Burke and, after the latter's retirement, she worked for Mrs. Marie (à Willie) Aucoin.

Mrs. Florence Mackley, a businesswoman of taste, owned a boutique in Sydney. She would buy rugs made in Chéticamp, making sure that she picked the most beautiful ones. She would have liked, however, to know one of the best rug makers whom she would have hired to work exclusively for her. Mrs. Marie Aucoin recommended Marie-Edna to her. From then on, for as long as Mrs. Mackley had her boutique, Marie-Edna made magnificent tapestries for her. The motifs which Marie-Edna designed were quite varied, featuring different kinds of flowers, beautiful seagulls and other birds, squirrels, etc. Furthermore, Marie-Edna had the ability to bring out in wool many nuances of colour which rendered her subjects most lifelike.

[See colour photo 28.]

In 1972, she was invited to exhibit some of her tapestries for a period of four days in the McConnell Memorial Library in Sydney. The showing was a great success and Marie-Edna's talent was most favourably praised in an article by Francis H. Stevens written for the *Sydney Post* [July 12, 1972].

Charlie Doucet (1914-1991)

Miss Burke's interest gave a boost to rug handcrafts which in turn led to a rise in personal initiative to design new motifs, which were jealously guarded by their designers.

Typical of these young artists was Charlie Doucet who, besides working regularly on large rugs for Miss Burke, amused himself by creating his own designs for his personal rugs. Two designs were dear to him. One of them was a representation of the schooner *Bluenose*, which he stamped on canvas himself and hooked with his aunt, Mrs. Adèle (à Stanislas dit Petit Coco) Deveau. The other design, ten square feet in area, featured a bouquet of roses with leaves, centred on a black background. This design was inspired by a similar one on a teacup.

Mr. Charlie Doucet

Charlie's rugs were very beautiful and quite a few other people wished they could have produced rugs of similar quality, but his aunt Adèle did not want him to stamp his designs for anybody else. She wanted his patterns kept for Charlie and herself.

One of Charlie's most beautiful rugs measured four square feet in area and featured a magnificent landscape with two fishermen on the banks of a river. One of them has a trout on his line while the other is poised to trap it in his dipper. The finish of this tapestry was such that one would have mistaken it for a painting.

His rugs did not gather dust for long in the boutiques. Tourists, who recognized the special quality of Charlie's rugs, bought them very quickly. Furthermore, Mr. Doucet also exercised his artistic talents in the fields of painting and photography.

Mrs. Christie-Anne (à John à Raymond) Poirier (1879-1931)

The people of Chéticamp who made rugs for Miss Burke trusted her judgment and diligently tried to abide by her discriminating tastes. These people felt indebted to her and were very careful not to disappoint her. Thus, if a rug was promised for a certain date, no efforts were spared to deliver it on time. In the anecdote which follows, Mrs. Christie-Anne Poirier, wife of John Poirier, supports this contention.

One day she was working on a rug which she was supposed to deliver the morning two days after; she realized that she did not have enough wool to finish it. The following morning, she got up at 5 o'clock and ran to the fields where she sheared a sheep. She washed the required amount of wool in hot water, dried it, and then picked out the impurities. She then carded the wool, spun it, dyed it, dried it one more time, and wound it into a ball. At midnight her rug was finished and could be delivered, as promised, the next morning. She had accomplished her task without ignoring the chores of cooking the meals and looking after the children.

The superb craftsmanship of Christie-Anne's rugs were proof of her artistic talents. She had made a 114-square-foot rug for Miss Burke, which represented a map of the world. In spite of the fact that the soft shades necessary made it difficult to reproduce the design, she did a very good job. Miss Burke paid her $114 for the rug. A few years later, Christie-Anne read in an American magazine that the automobile magnate, Henry Ford, had just bought a handmade rug, a veritable work of art representing a map of the world. The rug, for which Mr. Ford paid $4000, was destined to adorn his most beautiful yacht.

Therein lies proof of the profits which Miss Burke realized through the sale of Chéticamp hooked rugs. Christie-Anne was furious. She anxiously awaited the return of Miss Burke to Chéticamp to give her a piece of her mind. However, Cristie-

Anne died in 1931 before Miss Burke's arrival in Chéticamp.

Marie-Yvonne and Isabelle Muise

Mrs. Mathilde (à Simon) Muise made *breillon* rugs which she bartered for the pedlars' merchandise. Later she worked on woolen rugs for Mrs. Marie (à Willie) Aucoin, Miss Burke's agent.

Mrs. Muise was the mother of several children, two of whom were handicapped. Marie-Yvonne had club feet and Isabelle had a crippled back and hip. Except for Isabelle who attended school for a year, the two daughters did not have any schooling but were nonetheless very talented.

They began their apprenticeship with their mother but soon surpassed her in their workmanship. Soon thereafter, while still very young, they started to make their own rugs for Miss Burke. They did not let their mother work on the rugs, for they felt that her work was inferior to theirs.

Miss Burke remained satisfied with their rugs. Each time she came to Chéticamp she never failed to visit them. She would spend many hours with them encouraging them in their work. She never forgot to send them Christmas gifts.

In those days, there were no pensions for the handicapped. Courageous girls that they were, Marie-Yvonne and Isabelle earned their living by making rugs, although this work was arduous because of their handicaps. Thus, when in 1957 pensions became available to the handicapped, they were very grateful and stopped this kind of work, which was really demanding on them.

Marie-Yvonne died in 1961 at the age of 34; Isabelle died in 1966 at the age of 44.

Miss Antoinette Deveau (1892-1978)

At the age of five, Miss Antoinette Deveau contracted poliomyelitis which left her with both legs paralyzed; one of her legs never grew and Antoinette constantly kept it hidden by sitting on it. The other leg was sufficiently developed to allow Antoinette to move the chair on which she was always seated. Wheelchairs were not yet known in Chéticamp.

In spite of her handicap, Antoinette became a competent seamstress. Women would come to her and have a dress made according to a model they had seen in Eaton's catalogue, but they invariably requested a different collar or a different back. Antoinette always managed to satisfy their demands perfectly. She too became well known in Chéticamp for her hooked rugs.

Antoinette lived with her brother, Damien Deveau, and worked on rugs with her sister-in-law, Virginie. The latter dyed the wool, but Antoinette stamped the canvas and hooked the most difficult sections of the rug. She too earned her living by making rugs and by sewing.

Antoinette was one of the artists whom Miss Burke trusted to produce her most beautiful and often her most difficult rugs. A particular large rug featured apple trees in the fall with their faded and dried leaves, a few of them torn. The proper shading of colours was difficult to reproduce and to blend on a jute canvas. Antoinette was successful in reproducing this phenomenon, so much so that the leaves looked like they were ready to fall off the trees.

Antoinette also had a special talent for reproducing flowers with wool and a hook. These flowers were so lovely and real-looking that the people felt like plucking the petals.

When Miss Burke stopped buying rugs, Antoinette moved in with her sister, Mrs. Nanette (à Marcellin à Amédée) Aucoin, and from that point on, they worked together on rugs which, because of their particular beauty, were quickly bought by tourists.

Later on, Antoinette was able to benefit of an old age pension and a wheelchair. She spent her last years at Foyer Père Fiset where her services of seamstress were very much appreciated. She died there at the age of 86 in 1978 leaving behind memories of a jovial, sympathetic and very courageous woman, in spite of her handicap.

The Notorious Crisis of 1936-1937

Division among the "hookeuses"

The rug making business continued to grow during the years 1936-1937. New markets were opening up; Miss Burke continued to buy rugs at a very low price. When it was learned that she sold these rugs at a very high price thereby realizing at times a huge profit, discontent began to grow.

The cooperative movement had just started in Chéticamp. Study groups, which enabled the local people to discuss their economic problems, had been formed. Not much time elapsed before the question of rug making was tackled.

Alexandre Boudreau, agronomist for the region, devoted his efforts and time to bringing about an improvement in the living conditions of the Chéticamp citizens. Having been one of the principal architects in the founding of a credit union and a cooperative general store, he could not remain indifferent to the problems of rug making.

After several study sessions on the subject and encouraged by Mr. Boudreau, a group of rug makers decided to act, and circulated a petition asking Miss Burke to pay one dollar per square foot for the rugs. Charlie Doucet, who was mentioned earlier, agreed to visit the people who worked on the rugs to solicit their support by having them sign the petition. Everyone concerned was in favour of a higher price for their work, and the majority of the people agreed to sign the petition. Others, however, being more timid, refused to sign.

Miss Burke was offended by the petition and disagreed to the demand. The group which had signed the petition then sent her a telegram announcing that they would no longer work for her.

The people involved in the

Mr. Alexandre Boudreau

rug making business split into two groups: the one which remained faithful to Miss Burke and to her Chéticamp agent, Mrs. Marie (à Willie) Aucoin, and the other which decided to strike out on its own, with Mrs. Marie (à Charlie à Lubin) Aucoin as their agent. This split caused friction in a community where everybody knew everybody else, and much talk resulted. There were some squabbles. A rug which had been started for Miss Burke had to be moved to another house as the women who had started it decided to join the opposition.

All this commotion happened in winter while Miss Burke was in New York. Kept abreast of the developments by her friends, Miss Burke did not wait until summer to come to Chéticamp this time, but arrived in early March. She immediately went to Alexandre Boudreau's office to beg him to stop ruining her business. Mr. Boudreau did his best to make her understand that the people of Chéticamp who worked at rug making worked hard, needed money and were insufficiently paid for their labours.

Miss Burke was not interested in the arguments and she sued Mr. Boudreau and Mrs. Marie (à Charlie) Aucoin. The case was heard by Magistrate Lazare Boudreau. Miss Burke contended that the rugs made in Chéticamp were the result of her artistic work and consequently her property. Mr. Alex H. MacKinnon, a lawyer from Inverness who was hired by Mr. Alexandre Boudreau, encountered no problems in rebutting the plaintiff.

Miss Burke's last years

Miss Burke continued her visits to Chéticamp and did business with the people who had remained faithful to her. Because of the competition, she gradually had to raise the price that she paid for the rugs. She eventually paid one dollar per square foot, that which she had refused at first and which caused her to lose half of her labourers.

For all these reasons, Miss Burke was criticized by many in Chéticamp; at the same time she was liked and appreciated by many others. Miss Burke was generally recognized by everybody as having been the promoter of the rug making business, and it is because of her that the rug industry of Chéticamp enjoys its present reputation.

Miss Burke herself never made a hooked rug. One year she had to bring Marie-Antoinette (à Willie) Aucoin to New York to repair a rug which had unravelled loops here and there.

Nonetheless, Miss Burke was a great artist who invested her talents, her heart and much of her time to instill in the Chéticamp artisans an appreciation of the beautiful and to teach them how to express this appreciation through rug making. She taught them how to choose better colours, how to dye the wool, how to realize all the desired shades of colour, that the best wool is desirable, and finally how to produce rugs which are really high quality artifacts.

Miss Burke is to be appreciated for insisting that the rugs she ordered be to her demanding standards, for in so doing she taught the people who worked for her what is in good taste and instilled in them an appreciation of perfection.

She must have realized interesting profits with the Chéticamp-made rugs. It is incontestable that she did not pay sufficiently the people who worked hard at making rugs for her. She paid a very small fixed salary based on a square foot of rug and she in turn sold the rug at a high price depending on the overall value of the rug.

The rug making industry, like many others, slowed down with the start of World War II in 1939. Miss Burke never returned to Chéticamp. She took on a position at the New York Institute of Psychiatry where she was very successful because of her talents of psychologist and artist.[1]

Miss Burke died in 1952. She and her work are well remembered in Chéticamp. Chéticamp owes her its hooked rug industry and, it is worth repeating, is indebted to her for having developed this form of handcraft to a perfection which has achieved international renown. [See the tribute paid to Miss Burke by the Department of Trade and Industry of the Government of Nova Scotia, page 147.]

In spite of much research, the only photograph of Miss Burke which could be found was in an old yellowed 1937 issue of the *Sydney Post* which was kept by chance in a basement. Mr. Charlie Doucet put his knowledge of photography to use and retouched the photograph, eliminating two other people in the photograph, enlarging the rug which was visible in the background, and finally reproducing the photograph in colour—an unqualified success. *[See colour photo 2.]*

Mrs. Marie (à Willie à Helene) Aucoin (1890-1974)

Mrs. Marie (à Willie) Aucoin remained the leader of the group which was faithful to Miss Burke, even after the latter ceased doing business in Chéticamp.

Mrs. Marie (à Willie à Hélène) Aucoin

73

She would stamp the canvases, even the ones for the largest rugs. Having learned the basics from Miss Burke, she developed her natural artistic talents and made some beautiful rugs herself. She would spend hours on each flower in the pattern of the rug. The birds which she reproduced in wool looked so natural that they seemed alive. She was also very good at reproducing beautiful landscapes.

Her devotion to the ladies who worked for her was unwavering and she spared no pains nor her valuable advice. When Miss Burke gave up the business of rugs, Mrs. Aucoin opened a store in her own living room where she sold her clients' rugs to the tourists. Often she would ship large rugs to national exhibitions or to foreign buyers, painstakingly preparing them for shipment. Because of her kindness, at times she paid for rugs before production to help out some of the ladies in need of money who worked for her. She kept only ten percent of the price of the rug which was put up for sale in her store and to those who preferred to sell their rugs immediately, she paid one dollar per square foot. If she commissioned the production of a large rug, she also paid one dollar per square foot for the work.

After many years of devotion to the business of rug making Mrs. Aucoin, already advanced in years, ceased her involvement in this field, content to hook rugs for her own enjoyment and pastime.

She died in 1974 at the age of 84. Regretfully, none of her rugs nor any photographs of them are available today. Chéticamp owes her a large debt of gratitude for the enthusiasm and devotion that she dedicated to the expansion of the rug making industry.

1. Dr. G. B. Fairchild, *Cape Breton's Magazine,* Number 19, p. 47.

CHAPTER 10

Mrs. Marie (à Charlie à Lubin) Aucoin and the Dissenting Group

Mrs. Marie (à Charlie à Lubin) Aucoin—known in Chéticamp as Marie (à Luc)—worked for Miss Burke before the crisis of 1936. Her specialty was five-square-foot rugs featuring night scenes with a sailing ship at sea.

Mrs. Aucoin was an intelligent person, a woman of taste who, moreover, was very adept at dealing with people.

During the crisis of 1936, when the women working for Miss Burke split their loyalties, the dissident group turned to Mrs. Aucoin and insisted that she become their sales representative. After much hesitation and apprehension, she acceded to their demands and gradually became successful in this new endeavour.

This new group had worked out different terms of business. Mrs. Aucoin would get a ten percent commission of the sales of the rugs which were exhibited at her place during the summer for sale to tourists. For large rugs which she would commission, she would pay one dollar per square foot. She also accepted to buy rugs, for the same price as for the ones commissioned, from the ladies who wanted to sell to her directly, particularly in the wintertime because they needed the money.

Difficult beginnings

The first years turned out to be difficult ones. In spite of signs posted, it took a while before tourists discovered Mrs. Aucoin's home, now turned into a store.

To answer the needs of some of the women who worked for her and who wanted to sell their rugs directly to her because they needed the income, Mrs. Aucoin, over the course of several years, had to borrow considerable amounts of money from the Credit Union. She was such a likeable woman and the rugs she sold were of such beauty that the tourists who dealt with her, in effect, became her publicity agents. She sold only quality rugs, often retouching sections of the rugs that had been brought to her because they were not up to standards.

A large amount of work

Mrs. Aucoin bought jute canvas by the roll which she cut up in various sizes as required by the rugs to be made. She would stamp the designs on these canvases herself. She did this for most of the two hundred people whom she represented. She drew the designs on the canvas with a small stick which she dipped in ink or dye as determined by each line that she wanted to reproduce on the canvas.

She would stamp designs on small rugs on her kitchen table during the day. At night, when the day's work was done and the table cleared, she would put a sheet of plywood, four feet by eight feet, on the table and spread the canvas for a large rug over it. Patterns for a large rug were usually inspired by a small design which had to be applied to the large canvas according to scale. The time and patience required to reproduce a small scale model on a canvas of several hundred square feet featuring a complex and detailed motif staggers the imagination.

New markets

Within a few years, Mrs. Aucoin had opened new, interesting markets. She was helped in this endeavour by Mr. Auguste (à Damase) Deveau, a native of Chéticamp who worked in Montréal. During his summer holidays, he would often visit Mrs. Aucoin. He suggested that he bring back to Montréal some of the rugs in the hope of being able to sell them. Back in the metropolis, he approached two important organizations, the Canadian Handicraft Guild and Canada Steamship Lines. The rugs which he showed to these organizations were deemed to be too beautiful to possibly be the result of handcraft projects. Mr. Deveau had difficulty in convincing them that they were indeed so, but that having been done, the two organizations ordered many rugs which in turn they sold throughout Canada and the United States. Furthermore, Canada Steamship Lines embellished many salons of its ships with these rugs.

Mr. Auguste (à Damase) Deveau

These two organizations would order especially large rugs on which Mrs. Aucoin stamped the designs and then recruited the people necessary to complete the project. As was true of other large rugs, prototypes had to be finished before work could proceed on the original.

After a few years, Mr. Deveau ceased to function as the intermediary and asked the two organizations to deal directly with Mrs. Aucoin. Business continued with these two organizations and its volume increased over several years.

Other markets were developed in Canada, some as far away as Victoria, British Columbia, and the United States. Mrs. Aucoin was busy day and night. Two hundred people were working for her. Some people would hook small rugs all year long and in several houses a large rug was continually to be found mounted on a large frame. Before the war in 1939, money was scarce and fishing, the principal industry of Chéticamp, did not bring in enough revenue, as the fishermen got paid a penny a pound for the cod they caught. Men, women and

"Farm Yard Rug" measuring 70 square feet

children worked at rug making in order to earn some money. If in the years that followed Mrs. Aucoin realized some well deserved profits, her most genuine motivation always was to help these families with this extra source of revenue which she was making available to them.

New momentum

Obviously, the opening of new markets gave the rug making business extra momentum. Rugs were being shipped to exhibitions in Montréal, Toronto and New York. Their circle of fame was expanding. There were newspaper articles and radio programs about them. Eventually, the National Film Board and later the French and English branches of the CBC in the Atlantic Provinces produced several films, and on a few occasions aired programs, about this form of handcrafts.

The Montréal organizations which were mentioned previously ordered not only rugs and tapestries but also bedspreads and large curtains made in the same way as the rugs. For the curtains, these organizations would ship to Chéticamp a quality canvas which was to serve as the background material itself. Only the motifs were worked on the canvas. The stamping of the designs on these curtains was a delicate matter. The motifs of the left curtain had to correspond exactly to the motifs of the right curtain but they had to be in reverse order. Usually only a sketch of the design was sent to the artisans and the pattern had to be enlarged according to scale. Naturally, no stray line or ink could be visible on the canvas which served as background material.

In 1939, large curtains—which measured, when closed, thirteen feet in height and seventeen feet in width—were ordered by the Canadian Handicraft Guild for a Montréal theatre. Mrs. Aucoin stamped the design very carefully and, under her supervision, the curtains were made at Mr. Joseph (à Fabien) Deveau's. Lined with turquoise satin, they were magnificent. Mrs. Aucoin was invited to go to Montréal, all expenses paid, to supervise the installation of the curtains in the theatre. Unfortunately, other commitments prevented her from making the trip. [According to a letter from Olga Bauman, secretary of the Canadian Handicraft Guild, dated September 22, 1983, it was impossible to trace the name of this theater.]

The Church's rugs

Because of this new publicity concerning the rugs and their popularity, the people of Chéticamp were justifiably proud of their work. On the walls of many of their homes could be found very beautiful rugs featuring birds, landscapes and the schooner *Bluenose*.

In 1940, the people decided that they wanted to present the parish church with a rug worthy of this place of worship. Father Patrice LeBlanc gave his permission and agreed to pay for the canvas and the wool. The rug which measured thirty-three feet and four inches in length by two feet and three inches in width was set up on a frame at Mr. Joseph (à Fabien) Deveau's. Mrs. Marie (à Charlie) Aucoin stamped the design and dyed the wool. She also supervised the work of many volunteers who made the rug. After a month of continuous work, the rug was finished. When spread out, the rug started at the main altar and ran down the steps through the sanctuary all the way to the altar rail. It was a magnificent rug and very representative of the artistic talents of many of the faithful of the parish.

[See colour photo 18.]

Due to a lack of care, after a few years the rug was dirty and full of candle wax. Without consulting the ladies, Father LeBlanc had the rug removed. Mrs. Aucoin retrieved the rug, cleaned it and mended the worn sections, making the rug as good as new. For the procession on Corpus Christi, she spread the rug out in front of one of the altars of repose which was part of the procession route. Father LeBlanc was surprised to see it there, and looking so beautiful. Thus the rug regained its place in the church's sanctuary.

In 1957, the new curate, Father Jules Comeau, Eudist, had the interior of the church painted and the floor of the sanctuary covered with a red carpet. Once again the hooked rug had disappeared. It was found again in 1980 by Gérard and Annie-Rose Deveau. The rug had been cut in two. One section was laid out in front of the altar in the sacristy where it had become faded because of exposure to sunlight. The other section was lying about in a closet. This latter section was cleaned, repaired and laid by Father Fiset's tomb in the basement of the church.

Two other rugs, each ten square feet in area, were also found in the same closet. Their patterns had been stamped by Mrs. Aucoin and they had been made by Marie-Edna Roach. They had been presented to Father Jules Comeau on February 17, 1963, by les Dames de Sainte-Anne. The first featured Easter lilies; the second featured clusters of grapes. These two rugs were also cleaned by Gérard and Annie-Rose Deveau and they are now hanging as tapestries on the walls of Father Fiset's tomb.

The end of Mrs. Marie (à Charlie) Aucoin's business

Having become a widow in 1949, Mrs. Aucoin relied on the revenue from the sale of rugs for her living. In 1961, however, she married Mr. Willie Deveau and decided to end her association with the rug business which she now found too time consuming. The women begged her to continue, for without her, they felt that they would not be able to sell their rugs. Mrs. Deveau agreed to continue her commercial operation for a few more years.

By 1964, however, there were in Chéticamp several boutiques where the women could sell their rugs directly to the owner or leave them on consignment to be sold to the tourists. Mrs. Deveau gradually retired from the rug business.

For a period of thirty years, Mrs. Deveau had spent her energy in the rug business, showing much enthusiasm, devotion and talent. Because of her, the rug making business in Chéticamp underwent a new and phenomenal expansion. During this period of time, Mrs. Deveau met many people, and every summer quite a few tourists and friends continued to visit her.

Mrs. Deveau died December 1, 1989.

CHAPTER **11**

Some of This Handcraft's Renowned Artists

Several of these "artists in wool" have distinguished themselves either by the perfection of their work, by the originality of their designs, or by certain events which brought them into the spotlight. Several of the most prominent of these artists will be the subject matter of this chapter.

Mrs. Antoinette (à Paul) Lefort (1919-1994)

The excellence of her work qualifies Mrs. Antoinette (à Paul) Lefort to be among these distinguished artists. She will always be known for her beautiful tapestries which were impeccably done.

Born in 1919, she started her career in rug making at the age of eleven. The following year she was accepted to work on the large rugs being produced for Miss Burke and very

early, because of her exceptional talents, she was chosen to work on the more intricate designs of these rugs. Following this, Miss Burke, who recognized the particular talents of Antoinette, entrusted her with her most beautiful rugs and especially her new designs. In 1939, Miss Burke asked Antoinette to

Nova Scotia coat of arms held by Mr. and Mrs. Léo (à Stanislas) Boudreau

make her a tapestry nine by twelve inches featuring a beautiful bluebird. The model for this bird was taken from a book which featured various birds in colour. Antoinette reproduced this model so well that Miss Burke, who at that time was paying one dollar per square foot, gave her one dollar and twenty-five cents per square foot plus the book on birds. The bird depicted on this tapestry seemed to be alive and ready to take flight.

Antoinette continued reproducing these bird designs even after Miss Burke discontinued her visits to Chéticamp. These smaller rugs were selling for five dollars at a time when generally they would have sold for only two dollars per square foot.

[See colour photo 29.]

In 1940, Antoinette stamped the Nova Scotia coat of arms on a ten-square-foot canvas and hooked the detailed part of the design. Mrs. Maggie (à Léo) Cormier, who had received the order for this tapestry, hooked the easiest part, the background. Marie and Léo (à Stanislas) Boudreau had this tapestry commissioned so that they could hang it in the salon of their hotel in Chéticamp, The Ocean Spray. They paid ten dollars for it and a few years later sold it for one hundred dollars to an American tourist.

Starting in 1950, Mrs. Lefort, for several years, made ten-square-foot rugs for Mrs. Florence Mackley's store in Sydney. The revenue from these rugs helped support her family of ten. She worked very hard. She would get up at five in the morning and start her day working on the rugs, and in spite of her household chores, she found time to work on the rugs during the day and at night, up to midnight. Working at this rate, she would produce a ten-square-foot rug per week. Of course she dyed her own wool and stamped the canvases with her designs.

For a long time she placed her rugs for sale at Flora's Gift Shop, and she stamped the canvases of all the women who were suppliers of this shop as well as dyed their wool.

For several years, Mrs. Lefort was renowned for her magnificent Cap Rouge landscapes. Because these tapestries were so well known, the general public and the tourists demanded that she sign her works. Whenever tourists notice the name "Antoinette" in the corner of a tapestry, they buy it immediately even if it is more expensive than the others.

[See colour photo 27.]

Through the excellence and beauty of her work, Mrs. Antoinette Lefort was a motivating factor for the other rug makers, and thus she did and still does exercise a great influence on the quality of rugs made in Chéticamp.

Mrs. Marguerite-Marie (à Joseph à Den) Chiasson (1922-   )

Marguerite-Marie Bourgeois, now Mrs. Joseph Chiasson, started making *breillon* rugs at the age of twelve.

Those were the days of the pedlars; times were tough but the kindheartedness of the people could be counted on. One winter Marguerite-Marie and her mother made ten rugs, each being ten square feet in area. One of Marguerite-Marie's aunts, Mrs. Justile (à Amédée) Boudreau, who had a big family, was sick all winter. Marguerite-Marie and her mother brought her the ten rugs which she exchanged for clothes at Den Doucet's, where the pedlars left their merchandise for this kind of barter. This kind act enabled Mrs. Boudreau to dress all of her children for the winter.

Marguerite-Marie was not yet fifteen when she started working with her mother on the woolen rugs done with a hook as had been started in Chéticamp by Miss Burke. Her brother Gabriel stamped all their canvases, but in Marguerite-Marie's estimation he was too meticulous and took too long to do the job. She was always badgering him for not being fast enough. One day, tired of his sister's insistence, he shouted back at her, "Here, take all this and stamp them yourself, if you're capable," and he left the house. Marguerite-Marie had to finish stamping the design on that canvas. She did a very good job, and it can be said that from that moment on, she launched a career in stamping designs on canvas.

At fifteen she was stamping the canvases for several women; she also stamped a canvas one hundred square feet in area for Mrs. Florence Deveau's boutique, "Foyer du souvenir." For a long time she stamped canvases for Mrs. Marie LeLièvre's

Marguerite-Marie (à Joseph à Den) Chiasson

85

boutique, and did the same for Mrs. Bella (à Henri) Lefort for a period of twenty years. In the years that followed she devoted almost all of her time stamping designs for several boutiques in Chéticamp. These canvases vary from three inches in diameter (for coasters) to ten square feet in area for the largest rugs produced today in Chéticamp. As talented as Marguerite-Marie is in applying designs on canvas, she is equally talented in hooking beautiful rugs, for she has been making some since she was very young. For many years, like other women in Chéticamp, she sold her rugs to Mr. Harrison's boutique in Baddeck. Marguerite-Marie sold him coasters especially. She would make as many as two hundred of these in a month. At a selling price of twenty cents each, she earned forty dollars a month working at her craft, very often until midnight.

In 1970, Mr. Francis Coutelier, professor of visual arts at the University of Moncton, came to Chéticamp to give art courses. At the end of these courses, the professor held a contest among his students. The students were asked to produce a design, without the use of a model, which would feature at least eight different shades of grey. Marguerite-Marie won first prize with her four-square-foot design of interweaving circles. She then used this model for making a hooked tapestry which she placed for sale at the Coopérative artisanale. In less than two hours, the tapestry had been sold. Encouraged by her success, she went on to produce many tapestries which featured abstract designs and which always were popular sellers.

Marguerite-Marie is also known for the magnificent landscapes which she created with the hook. One winter she had hooked twenty-seven which she left in consignment for sale at Mrs. Bella Lefort's boutique. Hung together on a wall, the ensemble of these tapestries constituted a beautiful sight. Mrs. Lefort exhibited one of these landscapes along with other tapestries at an exhibition in Baddeck. Marguerite-Marie's tapestry won first prize.

Marie LeLièvre, for whom Marguerite-Marie stamped canvases, proposed to her that she create a simplified design for a tapestry featuring a tree with bilateral branches only, adorned with leaves. The tree was to be planted on a slight mound covered with grass. Marguerite-Marie stamped the design and hooked the tapestry herself. It was very beautiful and it sold immediately. This design is still being reproduced today. Some people add flowers or birds to the branches. It has been called "The Tree of Life." When Mrs. LeLièvre suggested this motif, she was far from suspecting that the resulting tapestry would become famous. It was precisely one of these tapestries made in Chéticamp which the Government of Nova Scotia presented as an official gift to Queen Elizabeth II during her visit to that province in 1976.

[*See colour photo 6.*]

Mrs. Catherine (à Jos à John) Poirier (1901-1994)

Mrs. Poirier— better known as Catherine à Mosé, and daughter of John (à Joseph) Cormier, of the parish of Saint-Joseph-du-Moine— always hooked rugs, having started with *breillon* rugs at a very early age. In 1925, she married Mosé Roach, son of Polite à Canivet. She lived with her husband at her father-in-law's place. Later in her life, after she became a widow, she married Jos (à John) Poirier.

Mrs. Catherine Poirier

Catherine Poirier is included among the notables of the rug making business especially because of the originality of the designs of her tapestries. In fact, too many people are content to reproduce designs which they find on photographs, postcards or paintings, which sometimes they modify a little. Catherine created her own designs and expressed them in an unsophisticated style which gives her work much charm.

Blessed with imagination and talent, she quickly achieved recognition in this kind of handcrafts. As early as 1940, taking her inspiration from a post card, she produced a twelve-square-foot rug. The motifs, much of which she expressed in her forthright style, featured roses and velvety spirals done in varied shades of green on a black background with a green border.

That year, the first busload of tourists came to Chéticamp after having previously announced their intended visit. The local ladies set up in the parish hall an exposition of rugs and tapestries for the benefit of these tourists and a prize was to be offered to the one who was judged as having the best work exhibited. The honour of selecting the winner was left to the tourists, and they chose Catherine's rug as winner of the prize. The tourists bought many of the works exhibited including the prize-winning rug.

This first visit of a busload of about forty tourists caused a sensation in Chéticamp. Catherine's father-in-law, Polite à Canivet, who had gone down to the harbour, returned home completely overwhelmed. He said to his wife, "The world has gone mad! A busload of people from God only knows where has arrived. They have bought all the rugs of the exhibition; and what is even more crazy, they have accorded first prize to Catherine's rug!" Deep down, he was a bit jealous for his own daughter, Adèle, who had also exhibited some beautiful works but had not won the prize.

In the years that followed, Catherine reproduced her prize-winning rug many times. The price she obtained for it increased with the years. In 1940 it sold for $11.50; in 1941 she got $13.50; in 1960 another one was sold for $70, and finally the last one, sold in 1969, brought in $100. In modern times (1983), the rug would probably sell for anywhere between two hundred and three hundred dollars. This valuable record of price, the only one we were able to find, gives an idea of how the prices have increased from the earlier days of this handcraft business to the present day.

Since 1979, Catherine specialized in small tapestries with simple designs featuring either the local church, the monument in commemoration of the fourteen founders of the village, boats, fishermen or barnyard birds. For example, one of her tapestries features a hen with her five chicks out for a walk at dusk. One chick to the left appears to be quite puny; another seems to be flaunting his independence; a third observes his mother scolding a fourth while the fifth one, to the right of the tapestry, is nonchantly looking for food.

[See colour photo 7.]

Mrs. Dorothy Harley Eber from Montréal and Mrs. Jane Mackeen Fagan from the United States each owned a summer home in Baddeck and had become good friends. One day while visiting Chéticamp, they found in a boutique one of Catherine Poirier's tapestries. They wanted to buy it, but it was already sold, so they inquired as to where Catherine lived and they went and visited her at home. Since that day, they buy practically all of Catherine's tapestries. After having collected several of Catherine's tapestries, in 1982 they mounted an exhibition of these works at the McCord Museum on Sherbrooke Street in Montréal. The exhibition started at the beginning of June and lasted until the end of December. Judging by the many people who visited the exhibition, it was a success.

Catherine was invited to go to the exhibition in October. At the age of 81, she travelled to Montréal accompanied by her sister. She was received like a queen. Radio and television people were present for the occasion. Catherine spoke candidly of her rugs and tapestries, told a story and sang a song. The program over, the sisters were invited to a reception at Mrs. Eber's where they were served champagne and hors-d'oeuvre.

On the way to Montréal by train, Catherine and her sister had slept together in a bed which was too narrow for two. Consequently, they had slept badly. For their return trip, Mrs. Eber paid for a roomette with two beds.

They returned delighted with their trip; they also had many orders for more tapestries.

Marie and Joseph-Léo Muise

Mr. Muise is the son of Simon (à Fred) Muise; Mrs. Muise is Marie (à Tanase à Placide) Larade. Marie and Joseph-Léo Muise both started working on rugs, like so many others, when they were very young. Since a few years, they have been selling all of their tapestries to the Warp and Woof Boutique owned by Mrs. Anne Flinn of Chester, Nova Scotia.

Marie and Joseph-Léo Muise

Mrs. Flinn visits Chéticamp every year on Good Friday. She too is a businesswoman of good taste. She usually arrives before the rugs and tapestries are shipped to other boutiques outside the village and she chooses the most beautiful ones.

In 1976, Mr. and Mrs. Muise produced a ten-square-foot rug featuring "The Tree of Life" motif, which was born out of an idea by Mrs. Marie LeLièvre and which has been described earlier in this chapter. It is interesting that in Chéticamp there are no copyrights on the designs in this field of handcrafts. Designs are copied from another person's shamelessly, so to speak. Nobody takes exception to this practice; everybody does it.

The rug "The Tree of Life," made by Mr. and Mrs. Muise, was bought by Mrs. Flinn for one hundred and twenty-five dollars. Since the Queen was visiting Nova Scotia that year,

Mrs. Flinn pro-
posed that the
Government of
Nova Scotia of-
fer the rug to
Her Majesty as
an official gift
from the Pro-
vince. Her pro-
posal was ac-
cepted.

The Muises,
having made
this rug, were
invited to the
official banquet
in Halifax where

"The Tree of Life" which was presented
to Queen Elizabeth II

the gift would be presented to the Queen.

Mrs. Muise being of a retiring nature did not want to
attend. She had never been to Halifax and had rarely been out
of Chéticamp. The ceremonies in which she was expected to
participate were disquieting to her. However, Élizabeth Lefort,
who was familiar with such experiences, called her to convince
her not to miss such a once-in-a-lifetime opportunity.

The Muises did make it to Halifax where Mr. and Mrs.
Flinn took them in charge and, being attentive to their task,
made things much easier for them. They were picked up at
their motel by a black limousine and driven to the Hotel Nova
Scotian where the banquet was taking place. Mr. Muise had
put on a formal jacket and his wife was wearing a formal gown.
They were seated at a table facing and very near the Queen.
From their vantage point they could admire at will the Sovereign
with her beautiful dress and royal crown.

The gift was presented to Her Majesty during the banquet.
It was wrapped up and had to be unwrapped for her. It was
announced that the gift was a rug but to the disappointment of

the guests, the rug was not shown to those attending the banquet.

After the banquet, Her Majesty made her way to the Muises to shake their hand and to congratulate them for the magnificent rug. She entertained the Muises in conversation for five minutes. The couple from Chéticamp had never felt so honoured or experienced such a thrill.

After the banquet, still travelling by limousine, the Flinns had them visit Halifax and its most important sites. They were then brought to the reception and ball given in honour of Her Majesty. The Muises were overpowered with the lavishness of the ballroom, the splendour of the music, the important personalities attending the dance, and the amount of liquor which was being served.

They, who had hesitated to accept the invitation to the presentation in Halifax, returned home, enraptured with their unique and unforgettable experience.

Paulite (à Paddée) (1909-   ) and Sadie Roach (1916-   )

Paulite Roach is the eldest of a family of fifteen. He had to leave school when very young to help his mother with the household chores.

He was very gifted and at a very early age he liked that all

Sadie and Paulite Roach

work should be well done. He appreciated and liked beautiful things. Thus when he started working on Miss Burke's large rugs, he was quickly noticed by her because of his excellent work. Often Miss Burke entrusted him with the most difficult sections of her large rugs. Eventually, she relied on him for her special rugs, the most beautiful ones, whose workmanship required the most talent and expertise.

In 1935, Polite married Sadie (à Charles) Gaudet who also worked on the rugs. They continued to work for Miss Burke. The economic depression of 1929 was unrelenting and created austerity and misery. In Chéticamp, the rug making business and fishing, for those who practiced these trades, were the only two sources of revenue. The ones involved in the rug making business were not well paid when their rugs were sold. This meant the tightening of one's belt and living poorly. Fortunately, Polite and Sadie owned a small farm which supplied them with vegetables. However, flour, sugar, salt, etc., which had to be bought at the local general store, were also necessary and quite often had to be bought on credit. Polite and Sadie brought up most of their thirteen children during these hard economic times. It was only later that they were able to enjoy relative affluence.

In 1938, Mr. Harvey, the man in charge of the logging camps at St. Ann's, Cape Breton, came to Chéticamp. He was interested in having an eighteen-square-foot hooked rug made. The rug was to feature the coat of arms of Canada and was to be Mr. Harvey's gift to the Governor General of Canada, John Buchan, Lord Tweedsmuir. At the Acadian Inn where he was staying, somebody referred him to Polite because of the perfection of his work. Polite accepted Mr. Harvey's request with joy. It was the first time that the Canadian coat of arms was to be reproduced in the form of a hooked rug. Polite stamped the canvas with meticulous care. Since the background was to be flecked, Sadie spun the wool and skeined it without doubling the strands. She then dyed some of the skeins beige and the others brown. Then she doubled the strands, using one of each colour, and wound it into a ball. When the resulting blend was used for the background, the latter had the desired mottled effect.

This rug was made at the home of Mrs. Annie (à Elie) Aucoin, daughter of Marcellin (à Hyacinthe) LeBlanc of the Cap Rouge district. Annie dyed the wool in the forty-six different colours necessary to reproduce the motifs. Annie worked on the background and Polite worked the design. He treated his work as a project of art. He would work a section of the design and like an artist would step back and appraise his work. Once finished the rug was exhibited at the Acadian Inn for several days where many people came to admire this masterpiece. For their work, the authors received one hundred dollars, which was a considerable sum for those days.

In 1945, Polite received a letter from Mr. G. E. Wills, a Canadian living in Florida. He had seen a photograph of the coat of arms tapestry in an American magazine, and he wanted a similar one made. Polite and his wife proceeded to do so and later shipped him the tapestry along with a bouquet of forty-eight strands of wool—one of each colour used in the tapestry. Later, Mr. Wills sent them a photograph of his family with the tapestry. In the photograph, Mr. Wills is holding the bouquet of wool strands in one hand.

Mr. Wills later commissioned a six-square-foot tapestry of the family's coat of arms which featured a dragon. He also commissioned for his friends quite a few more coats of arms of Canada and Nova Scotia.

In 1952, a tapestry featuring Nova Scotia's coat of arms was commissioned by the Handcraft Department of the Province's Ministry of Industry and Commerce. A photograph of this tapestry was published in 1955 in *Handcrafts in Nova Scotia*. This particular tapestry was often on exhibition in the major hotels of Halifax as well as in the Victoria General Hospital. In 1979 Mrs. Flinn, owner of the Warp and Woof Boutique of Chester, commissioned a similar tapestry which she offered to the Honorable G. L. Gosse, Lieutenant Governor of Nova Scotia, upon his retirement.

Polite and Sadie have had many requests for tapestries featuring the American flag as well as many others, all very difficult to realize but always successfully managed. The variety of their work is truly immense and their reputation as artists is known throughout North America.

[See colour photo 23.]

They are renowned for their tapestries, which feature the schooner *Bluenose* and magnificent landscapes, particularly picturesque Peggy's Cove. In June 1983, the Province's official gift to Prince Charles and Princess Diana was a tapestry featuring Peggy's Cove. Its authors, Polite and Sadie, were given the honour to be present at the presentation of the tapestry to the Royal Couple.[1]

[See colour photo 12.]

This occasion was the height of the careers of these two artists who throughout the years have made rugs and tapestries for renowned people, companies and important hotels of North America.

Mrs. Marie-Stella (à Louis-Léo) Bourgeois (1934-   )

Marie-Stella's mother—Marguerite, wife of Joseph (à Jim) LeBlanc—continually had a large rug mounted on which she and a group of ladies worked for Miss Burke.

As early as age four, Marie-Stella liked to imitate the ladies. They let her play with strands of wool and a hook on the border of a rug; they simply unravelled her "work" when they reached that section.

On one occasion when Miss Burke was visiting this group of workers, she found Marie-Stella imitating the ladies. Always the agreeable one, Miss Burke made a small frame out of pieces of wood, tacked on a canvas with thumbtacks, and drew a schooner on the canvas. She gave the whole ensemble to Marie-Stella so that she could play.

The four-year-old-child hooked her small rug. When Miss Burke returned for a second visit that summer, she was impressed enough with Marie-Stella's work that she took the

Mrs. Marie-Stella (à Louis-Léo) Bourgeois

small rug with her to New York. The following year when she returned to Chéticamp, she gave ten dollars to Marie-Stella's mother. She intended to exhibit Marie-Stella's small schooner along with other Chéticamp rugs.

Marie-Stella attended the local school and later earned her diploma in nursing. She then moved to Toronto where she stayed until she was twenty-three years of age. She then returned to Chéticamp with her husband, Louis-Leo (à Cyrille) Bourgeois.

During her years of schooling and her sojourn in Toronto, Marie-Stella had not been interested in hooked rugs. Upon her arrival in Chéticamp, her interest in hooked rugs was revived and her immense talent was soon evident. She produced magnificent tapestries of the Cabot Trail, Margaree Valley, Peggy's Cove, Blue Rocks and the Nova Scotia coat of arms, etc. Her tapestries were very popular in the local boutiques and she received numerous personal orders.

Her husband Louis-Léo, who had become the manager of the local Cooperative General Store, had many occasions to play host to representatives of the cooperative movement of the Maritimes. When these people saw Marie-Stella's work, they encouraged her to form a cooperative to sell hooked rugs and tapestries. Eventually, Marie-Stella and a few other women started the Coopérative artisanale. [See further along, in the chapter "The Boutiques," page 120.]

Marie-Stella thrives on challenges. Nothing seems impossible to her. As soon as a new idea comes to her mind, she has to try it out and invariably she succeeds. She is an accomplished seamstress; she's adept at pottery-making and sculpting; she knows how to weave, how to work with copper and how to stuff birds.

One day as she was walking on the beach, she noticed some small flat stones. She had the idea of turning them into brooches. She gathered several and painted a landscape on each. These pictures were so small that she had to use a toothpick instead of a paint brush to accomplish her task. She then glued these stones on a fastening mechanism, which gave her instant brooches!

However, it was the craft of hooked rugs that gave her the greatest challenge. It is generally known that to reproduce a face which looks like the real person is a very difficult task even when using the medium of paints. One badly outlined feature or an errant brush stroke and the resemblance disappears. Very little imagination is required to be able to grasp how difficult it must be to reproduce a face with a hook and wool. Élizabeth Lefort, who will be discussed later, is famous for her success with portraits "in wool." Marie-Stella decided to try her hand at portraiture as well.

In 1963, she started a twenty-four-square-foot tapestry reproducing Leonardo da Vinci's "Last Supper," Christ seated at a table with his twelve disciples. Thirteen figures was quite a challenge for a first attempt!

She stamped the canvas, dyed the wool and started to hook the tapestry. Eighteen months later, the tapestry was completed and was very beautiful indeed. However, the unfortunate events which are part of the story of this tapestry are sufficient in themselves to make a celebrity out of its author.

In 1966, Marie-Stella was invited to attend an exhibition in Toronto where she was to exhibit her tapestry and a few other rugs from the Coopérative artisanale. The articles to be exhibited were shipped three weeks in advance to the Canadian

National Guild of Toronto which was to judge which of them were worthy of exhibition. Those judged worthy were then to be forwarded to the Canadian National Exhibition. All articles were judged by experts. A judge from Paris disqualified Marie-Stella's tapestry on the grounds that it could not have been a genuine handcraft, that is literally made by hand.

When Marie-Stella arrived in Toronto, she was very disappointed to learn that her tapestry had not qualified for exhibition because one of the experts had made an error in his judgment. She would have loved to tear apart the judge from Paris but he had returned home. She was not that affluent and shipping her tapestry, which was framed and weighed one hundred and twenty-five pounds, had already cost her two hundred dollars. The Canadian National Guild was paying only part of her expenses, allowing for twenty-five dollars per day for three days. She had to pay for her own travelling expenses. As she did not have enough money left to have recourse to legal advice, she decided to defend the cause of her tapestry her way.

She managed to find a hot plate and containers which she used to dye some wool. She then stamped a design on canvas and proceeded to hook a rug sample for the people in charge of the exhibition, thus proving to them that her tapestry had indeed been done by hand. Faced with this obvious proof, the people in charge of the exhibition marvelled at her talent and allowed her to exhibit her tapestry at the Canadian National Exhibition. However, she would not be permitted to put a price on her tapestry or give too many explanations on how it was produced. All this happened on the eve of the exhibition.

By telephone, Marie-Stella rented a truck to transport her tapestry from the Canadian National Guild, where she was staying, to the Queen Elizabeth Building, some seven kilometres away where the exhibition was taking place. The truck which was rented to her was a milk delivery truck with a sliding door on one side. She had great difficulty in getting her twenty-five-square-foot tapestry into the truck. She had not hired anybody to drive the truck and she was not used to driving in Toronto, much less driving a milk delivery truck. She was so upset however that, as she said, she could have driven an airplane. Once exhibited, her tapestry was very much appreciated. The people were delighted when they saw such beautiful work.

Marie-Stella returned to Chéticamp where she exhibited her tapestry for a few years at the Coopérative artisanale. In 1969, she moved with her family to Montréal, taking along her tapestry.

In Montréal, the family took residence in the parish of Saint-Camille which has a beautiful church, built like a theatre. At the invitation of the parish priest, Marie-Stella exhibited her tapestry of "The Last Supper" in the church. She gave the parish priest a document which gave information about the tapestry. She wanted this document placed below the tapestry but her wish was ignored. Bad luck stayed with the tapestry. One day she saw a picture of it in a newspaper; her initials were clearly visible in one corner. The photograph had been taken in Saint-Camille church, but the caption below the photograph read: "A work of art done in needlepoint by Mrs. Archambault."

Once again deprived of recognition, Marie-Stella felt like taking the reporter to court. But dogged by bad luck, she had been in an automobile accident a few days before. She had emerged from the accident with a sore back, but her mother, who had been with her, was in a coma in the hospital. She dropped her plans to sue but she went and got her tapestry. She then exhibited it in the hospital where she worked.

In 1983, Marie-Stella brought her tapestry to Chéticamp so that it could be on permanent exhibition at the newly-opened Élizabeth Lefort Gallery. However, in the early 1990s, "The Last Supper" was purchased by the family of Joseph à Gabriel Doucet, who in turn presented St. Joseph's Parish with the tapestry for its permanent exhibition in the newly-built parish church.

Marie-Stella has hooked other portraits. The list includes John F. Kennedy, his wife Jacqueline, and Bing Crosby. These were sold in the United States and as a consequence Marie-Stella received many orders for similar tapestries. However, since

1969, Marie-Stella has concentrated on her work as a nurse in Montréal and has discontinued her involvement with handcrafts.

Marie-Stella, unfortunately, had another bad experience in connection with rugs. Her mother had been given some beautiful patterns for rugs by Miss Burke. Marie-Stella was preciously keeping these patterns in a small black suitcase. One day, in Montréal, when there was nobody home, burglars broke into the house and stole several objects, including the black suitcase containing Miss Burke's patterns. Marie-Stella was so grieved by this news that she almost became ill. Fortunately, a few days later, the police found the black suitcase in a river. The patterns had been left in the suitcase and although they were somewhat damaged they were still usable. The thieves who had hoped that the suitcase contained money were obviously disappointed. To Marie-Stella these patterns given to her mother by Miss Burke were worth more than a treasure.

All these incidents which seem to be taken from a work of fiction have generated much sympathy for Marie-Stella and much admiration for her tapestry, "The Last Supper," deemed by so-called experts to be too well crafted to qualify as a handcraft—which it certainly was.

Mrs. Élizabeth Lefort-Hansford (1914-2005)

When she was still a very young girl, Élizabeth Lefort—daughter of Placide (à Eusèbe) Lefort—learned how to make hooked rugs from her mother. At the beginning she worked with customary patterns, but she preferred to reproduce landscapes.

In 1940, one of her sisters asked Élizabeth to make a tapestry which she would give to one of her friends. At that time, Élizabeth had not yet begun to create her own designs, but she favoured a particular Christmas card which she had received. The card featured a barnyard scene with five sheep and four ducks. Élizabeth reproduced this scene on a piece of canvas, twenty-five inches by thirty inches, and dyed the wool

Mrs. Élizabeth Lefort-Hansford   Mr. Kenneth Hansford

for making the rug into twenty-eight shades of brown. This tapestry was so successfully reproduced that it launched its author on a career which made her famous and internationally renowned. [A sample of this tapestry, found in 1983, is exhibited in the Élizabeth Lefort Gallery.]

She reproduced this scene several times in the years that followed. Because of its beauty it sold for fifty dollars. It was this tapestry which was to bring about her introduction to a Toronto businessman, Kenneth Hansford, who would guide her work to the point of its becoming great art, and would also win for Élizabeth immense publicity.

Mr. Kenneth Hansford first visited Cape Breton as a tourist with his family around 1936-1937. He returned in September of 1938 to fetch his son, who had been convalescing during the summer at the Duck Cove Inn in Margaree. Attracted by this part of the country and sensing the tourist potential of the region, he bought a piece of land at Margaree Harbour in 1951. There he built a handcraft and souvenir store which he called the Paul Pix Shop.

Occasionally, Mr. Hansford would visit Chéticamp to buy hooked rugs for his boutique. On a stormy day when there were no tourists about, he came to Chéticamp. Fate brought him to Élizabeth Lefort's door. She showed him several of her works among which was the barnyard scene mentioned earlier. An accomplished photographer himself, Mr. Hansford immediately recognized Élizabeth's exceptional talent. He bought all her rugs and reserved all of the ones that she was to produce thereafter. He had the landscape framed and sold it shortly thereafter for $200. He had bought it for $45.

Hooked portrait of Mr. Dwight Eisenhower

When he visited Élizabeth again, he offered her extra money for the tapestry which he had sold at a considerable profit. She said to him, "Good for you if you have made money with it, but I have already been paid." Mr. Hansford nonetheless shared the profit with her.

In the years that followed, Mr. Hansford hired Élizabeth each summer to work in his souvenir shop for $50 a week. He set her up in a beautiful studio where she hooked all day long on her rugs, demonstrating her art to interested tourists. He also had a gallery built where Élizabeth's tapestries were exhibited. The gallery was an immediate success.

From this point on, Mr. Hansford became Élizabeth's manager, taking charge of the direction of her work and counselling her in her choice of motifs. He also developed a strategy to publicize Élizabeth's work. Amazed by the artist's genius, he wanted her work to be known world-wide.[2] Élizabeth herself admits that "without Mr. Hansford's interest she would probably have, all her life, produced insignificant rugs which she would have tried to sell to tourists."[3] Her career was much more than that.

In 1955, Mr. Hansford asked Élizabeth if she could produce a portrait with a hook and wool. She had never tried. He proposed that she try hooking a portrait of Dwight Eisenhower, then President of the United States. After much experimentation and starting over several times, she accomplished the task beyond her highest expectations.

Mr. Hansford, who spent winters in Phoenix, Arizona, brought the portrait with him in 1957 and, because of the influence of the former Governor of Arizona, Howard Pyle, then Eisenhower's assistant, he managed to have himself and Élizabeth invited to go to the White House and present the portrait to the President himself. That was Élizabeth's first experience with flying. Later Élizabeth received a letter from the President which stated: "I am keenly interested in the unusual effects that you are able to create through the medium of hand hooking in wool yarn."[4]

When Mr. Hansford and Élizabeth learned that Queen Elizabeth II was to visit Canada in 1959, they decided to present her with her portrait hooked in wool. It took Élizabeth only eleven days to produce this portrait, which measured twenty-seven inches by thirty-three and a half inches and which featured fifty different shades of colour. It was presented to Her Majesty in Sydney on July 31, 1959. The Queen seemed very pleased and had the tapestry transported immediately to her yacht in Halifax. When she returned to England, she took the tapestry with her which since then has been hanging in Buckingham Palace in London.

That same year, Élizabeth hooked the portrait of Pius XII, the Sovereign Pontiff. They wanted to present him with the portrait. Having made the Vatican aware of their intentions, the Chancellery of the Diocese of Antigonish was notified by Rome to check to see if the intention was serious and if the tapestry was legitimate.

The Bishop's Delegate, Father A. J. MacLeod, was simply astonished by the beauty of this tapestry. He suggested that it be presented to the Apostolic Delegate, Monseigneur S. Baggio, who in turn would present it to the Sovereign Pontiff. His suggestion was realized and the tapestry has been exhibited in the Vatican Art Gallery ever since.

When Pope John XXIII succeeded Pius XII, Élizabeth also hooked the new Pontiff's portrait. The portrait measured twenty-seven inches by twenty inches and required thirty-one different shades of wool. This tapestry also was magnificent. It was bought by the Catholic Women's League in Toronto and was given as a gift to Cardinal McGuigan of the same city. It was a reproduction of this tapestry which Élizabeth donated to the University of Moncton when she received her honorary doctorate degree in 1975.

On her first attempt, Élizabeth had proven her extraordinary talent in the difficult art of reproducing portraits in wool. Since then she has hooked the portrait of many other celebrities including that of U.S. President Johnson; Jacqueline Kennedy in 1962, which in itself is a masterpiece containing one hundred and six colours, fifteen of which were necessary for the face only; John Diefenbaker, Prime Minister of Canada; Lord Beaverbrook; Arthur Godfrey seated on his favourite horse; and Prince Charles. The latter portrait was intended to be presented on the occasion of his wedding, but attempts to have this accomplished through official channels only resulted in categorical refusal. Mr. Hansford then wrote directly to the Prince, who replied immediately that "he appreciated their thoughtfulness and that he would be pleased to accept the portrait."[5] The gift was sent to him by airplane. More than likely, that portrait is also exhibited in Buckingham Palace.

One of Élizabeth Lefort's masterful works is a tapestry featuring the Presidents of the United States and important events which occurred during their stay in the White House. Produced during the years of 1959 and 1960, it measures six feet three inches high by ten feet and three inches wide. It is evaluated at $100,000. The tapestry is entitled: "My Country, 'Tis of Thee."

At the centre of the tapestry is the President's seal and the official seal of the United States, symbols of law and governmental authority. The portraits of the first ten presidents, in the upper left corner, are blended into a background featuring Independence Hall. The portraits of the next ten presidents, in the upper right corner, are blended into a background featuring the battle of Antietam during the Civil War. The following six presidents, in the lower left corner, are blended into a background featuring a railroad car, symbol of the development of the American West. The six others, on the lower right, were each President during either of the World Wars; they oversee the capturing of the Remagen Bridge on the Rhine by the Americans. Finally, in the centre, underneath the two seals, Presidents Eisenhower and Kennedy are featured against the launching of a rocket into a beautiful night sky with the moon symbolizing hope. The border of this tapestry of all of the American Presidents and the highlights of their careers features the coats of arms of the fifty American States.[6]

The making of this tapestry required a picture of each of the presidents as well as research and study of their biographies and of the history of the United States. The layout of these portraits with their supporting background scenes required much creative imagination, and the realization of this tapestry was a veritable tour de force.

This tapestry in fact comprises thirty-four historical figures which required three hundred and ninety colours. The wool (two strands) required to complete the rug would cover a distance of 11.27 kilometres (7 miles), and 1,700,000 loops were made with the hook. Above all, "the details of this tapestry are of an incredible perfection which makes the tapestry a wonder of the artistic world."[7]

In 1962, Élizabeth produced a series of portraits, those of the first seven American astronauts—Alan E. Shepard, Virgil Grissom, John H. Glenn, Scott Carpenter, Walter Schirra,

Gordon Cooper and Donald Slayton. These portraits, 17 by 20 inches, contain anywhere from twenty to sixty different shades of colour. This collection is now exhibited in the Élizabeth Lefort Gallery at Les Trois Pignons in Chéticamp.

One of the tapestries, featuring the church at Grand-Pré and the statue of the Acadian heroine Évangéline, was presented to the President of France, General de Gaulle, by a party of four Acadians—Dr. Léon Richard, Gilbert Finn, Euclide Daigle and Adélard Savoie—who were on an official visit to France.

Élizabeth also made a tapestry in commemoration of the Dispersion of the Acadians in 1755. This tapestry comprises twenty-seven different characters and required one hundred and twenty different shades of wool to complete.

In 1967, Canada celebrated the centennial of its Confederation. To commemorate this occasion, Élizabeth produced another magnificent tapestry. This sixty-square-foot tapestry is the representation of important events in Canadian history. The upper third of the tapestry, from left to right, features John Cabot landing on Cape Breton Island in 1497; Jacques Cartier and the American Indians at Gaspé in 1534; the first canal built, linking the St. Lawrence and the Great Lakes; and finally Captain Vancouver surveying English Bay, the future site of the city of Vancouver. The lower third, at the left, features the gold rush in the Klondike in 1890, and to the right the successful passage to the North West by the Royal Canadian Mounted Police in 1944, on the ship *Saint-Roch*. In the middle of the lower third, the coat of arms are featured with the Peace Tower in Ottawa on one side and the monument in Vimy, France, on the other. The middle third features the Fathers of Confederation assembled to ratify the British North America Act which made Canada a confederate country under the jurisdiction of a federal government. Each of the scenes on this tapestry is a marvel of perfection.

This tapestry also features the portraits of the Prime Ministers of Canada during its first one hundred years of confederation (1867-1967). Finally, the border comprises the emblems of each of the Canadian provinces. This tapestry required 416 different shades of colour, nearly two million loops with the hook, and more than seven months for its author to complete.

[See colour photo 39.]

All these works would suffice to justify calling their author the "great Canadian artist in wool" as she was called by a journalist from Arizona.[8] Élizabeth, however, made many other tapestries, over three hundred, featuring pastoral scenes, animals, birds, etc., which tourists bought as quickly as they became available. One of these tapestries featuring a magnificent bird was presented as a gift by the Province of Nova Scotia to the Queen of England's mother when she visited Halifax in 1967.

Furthermore, Élizabeth created another collection of tapestries of incomparable beauty: a series on the life of Jesus. The series comprises the following: Jesus as an infant, Jesus the adolescent, an especially beautiful work, Jesus as an adult, The Last Supper, Calvary and the Resurrection. Each of these tapestries *[see colour photos 1, 37 and 38]* in this series is worthy of further study and of the greatest praise, even if they do not have the distinction of being original designs like many of Élizabeth's other tapestries. In fact this series is the reproduction in wool of some of the creations of the masters of the art world.

"The Last Supper," modeled on the famous painting by Leonardo da Vinci, measures eight feet by four and one half feet and required 154 colours. Of all her tapestries, Élizabeth favoured this one as her masterpiece. However, the tapestry depicting the scene on Calvary may be more beautiful. It covers 55 square feet of area and features 78 different characters and required 510 different colours to complete. It is a large portrait beaming with colour and light, startling in its realism. The largest in this series is the Resurrection, which covers an area of eighty square feet and required more than two million loops made with a hook.

Looking at these large tapestries with their extraordinary

craftsmanship and beauty, one cannot help but bring to mind the famous tapestries of the Gobelins of Paris.

It is therefore not surprising that the studio at the Paul Pix Shop and, from 1974 on, a more rustic building (an old barn also transformed into a pleasant studio) where this great artist worked, attracted each summer up to one hundred and fifty busloads of tourists, and visitors by the thousands in cars. Some came from as far away as Europe, Russia, South Africa and Australia.[9]

To make her marvellous tapestries, Élizabeth used the finest wool from Cape Breton sheep. However, certain sections of her tapestries, such as the Queen's dress, the shirt collars of the Presidents and the Sovereign Pontiffs' capes, required a pure white wool. A special angora wool from England was used to answer that requirement.

Naturally, Élizabeth dyed the wool in the shades necessary for her tapestries. She had the great ability of being able to obtain exactly the shade of colour she required. She also stamped her own canvases, a procedure which required enlarging according to scale and precise measurement. When the designs, which always required much study beforehand, were drawn on canvas, and when the wool had been dyed in the hundreds of shades of colour required, Élizabeth considered her tapestry practically completed. Hooking the rug, to her, seemed the easiest part to accomplish.

Because of her talent and training, Élizabeth could hook 55 loops in a minute, 3,300 in an hour, 26,400 in an 8-hour day and 158,400 in six days. When she presented the portrait to Her Majesty in 1959, Élizabeth told her that the portrait represented eleven days of work to which the queen answered to the point: "Eleven days of work, but no doubt a lifetime of experience."[10]

A description of Élizabeth Lefort's personality is an appropriate ending to this section devoted to the one who became Mrs. Kenneth Hansford in 1967 after the latter was widowed.

Even though she met some of the most important

personalities of the world, even though they received her with enthusiasm and welcomed her as a great artist, even though she was present at important exhibitions and attended magnificent social receptions, even though she was acclaimed by people in high places and received an honorary doctorate degree from the University of Moncton in 1975, Élizabeth did not let all this fame go to her head. She did not lose any of her unaffectedness and she was as warmly receptive as ever, as would be expected from her Acadian heritage. Poised, distinguished, and not intimidated by impressive occasions, she was always friendly, cordial and without pretension, like the young girl she was in 1940.

Because of her unaffectedness, she was admired by all, particularly by her compatriots of the Chéticamp region, who are very proud of her, and for whom she has always been an inspiration in their striving for better craftsmanship in the art of tapestry making. As testimony to this appreciation, an art gallery which was opened at the cultural centre Les Trois Pignons on August 7, 1983,[11] was named after her. The most beautiful pieces of her collection have been on permanent exhibition since the opening of the gallery.

Élizabeth Lefort was presented with the Order of Canada on April 29, 1987, in recognition of her ambassadorial work in the promotion of our Acadian culture, as well as her success in turning the local rug hooking industry into an art. Her contribution to the preservation of our Acadian culture and heritage, through the creation of original and magnificent tapestries, has been tremendous.

Annie-Rose (1927-   ) and Gérard Deveau (1922-1998)

Mr. Gérard (à Jos à Damase) Deveau started working on rugs when he was sixteen years old. After spending a few years in Halifax, he returned to Chéticamp to become an employee of the Cape Breton Highlands National Park. In 1948 he married Annie-Rose Poirier, daughter of Pitre à Midouche Poirier. Both of them have contributed to the industry of rug making. They are ardently devoted to this form of handcrafts. In 1981 Mr. Deveau retired as an employee of the Park and devoted most of his time to this craft until his death in 1998.

Both have produced masterpieces; both gave courses in this form of handcrafts. Gérard devised a way of improving the frames on which the large rugs are mounted so that they are more practical. Following is an account of their achievements in this field of handcrafts.

In 1967, the Coopérative artisanale received an order for thirty small rugs which were to cover the steps of the staircase in a historical house in Mount Uniacke. These rugs had to be particularly well made because of their illustrious destination— the country home of Richard John Uniacke, renowned lawyer for the government of Nova Scotia during the years 1797 to 1830. Built between 1813 and 1815, thirty-five kilometres from Halifax, this house was designated a historical site by the province of Nova Scotia.

Mr. and Mrs. Gérard Deveau, already renowned for the excellence of their work, were given the job of making these thirty rugs measuring two feet two inches by one foot each. They all featured the same pattern: roses in the corners with leaves on a beige background.

Needless to say, these rugs were successfully made and, even if thousands of tourists trample them each year, they are still in perfect condition after more than thirty-five years of use.

In 1972, an American scientist, Mr. John Mudge, came to Nova Scotia to photograph a solar eclipse and thereby obtain more precise data on this phenomenon. It was Mr. Mudge's first visit to Nova Scotia and to satisfy his curiosity he read much of the literature informing tourists of the particular interests of that part of Canada. It was thus that he happened on an article describing the hooked rugs of Chéticamp. When he returned home, he wrote to the Coopérative artisanale ordering a very special rug, made up of squares, each featuring a different motif which was symbolic of his career.

A star would represent his interest in astronomy; the fleur-

Annie-Rose and Gérard Deveau

de-lis would represent his many friends in France; a lion would be a symbol of his birth in England; an eagle would represent his American citizenship; a compass card would symbolize his many voyages; an anchor would represent his many years in the British Merchant Marine; cannons would represent his years of service as an officer of the artillery in the American army; and finally, on the border, symbols representing the Morse code signals identifying the special ships on which Mr. Mudge sailed the seven seas.

The background colours chosen for this rug were red and blue, the first symbolizing the spilt blood of the war and the second symbolizing peace. The rug was to cover an area of twenty-four square feet measuring four feet by six feet.

[See colour photo 26.]

Mr. and Mrs. Gérard Deveau were given the task of making this rug. When Mr. Mudge received it, he immediately expressed his admiration, praise and thanks in a letter. Mrs. Deveau, who at the time was preparing an album on Chéticamp hooked rugs for the cultural centre Les Trois Pignons, requested of Mr. Mudge a photograph of the whole rug as well as one of each

111

square comprising the rug. In 1980, then 80 years old, Mr. Mudge came to Nova Scotia for a second time. He travelled to Chéticamp to see this album and to meet the artisans who had produced his rug. After Mr. Mudge's death in 1987, this rug was returned to La Société Saint-Pierre. It is on permanent exhibition in the Élizabeth Lefort Gallery at Les Trois Pignons.

In 1980, to commemorate the 375th anniversary of the founding of Port Royal, the Acadian Federation of Nova Scotia decided to have a rug made which would emphasize this event. Since this anniversary of the founding of Acadia would be celebrated in many towns and villages of the province, the rug would be exhibited during each of these various celebrations. Because of its purpose, this rug had to be of a very high quality. Mr. and Mrs. Deveau were asked to make it.

The rug, featuring 88 different shades of wool, was to cover an area of thirty square feet and was to bear, in its centre, the inscription: "En Acadie, on est venu c'est pour rester."

Mr. Deveau stamped the canvas and hooked the most difficult sections himself; Mrs. Deveau dyed the necessary wool. As time was of the essence, the year already being 1980, Mr. and Mrs. Deveau had the best of the students to whom they were teaching rug hooking that year work on the remainder of the rug (709,500 loops), while supervising the work very closely.

[See colour photo 19.]

The unveiling of this magnificent rug took place in the Province's capital, Halifax, and was introduced to the public by its creators at a press conference which marked the official opening of the celebrations. During that anniversary year, the rug was circulated throughout the province and was returned to Chéticamp, where the closing ceremonies of the celebrations of the 375th anniversary took place. The beauty of the rug was admired everywhere. Because the rug is the property of the Acadian Federation of Nova Scotia, it is on exhibit at that society's headquarters in Halifax when it is not on loan to some other exhibition.

It was not without regret that the people of Chéticamp

gave up this masterpiece. La Société Saint-Pierre commissioned a similar tapestry, but half the size of the original. Mr. and Mrs. Deveau went to work a second time, helped by Mrs. Henriette Aucoin and Mrs. Marie-Rose Deveau. This rug was to be on permanent exhibition at Les Trois Pignons. In order to recognize the original's singularity, it was decided to replace the motto "En Acadie, on est venu c'est pour rester" by the number "375th." The second rug was also done in 1980 and when the Acadian Federation of Nova Scotia learned that the Governor General of Canada, Mr. Ed Schreyer, was to take part in the celebrations, the Society decided to buy this second rug and present it to His Excellency as a worthy and appropriate souvenir of the celebrations.

Once again Les Trois Pignons was without the rug. The four people who had made the second one made a third of the same size, changing a few things. The number "375th" in the centre was kept but was surrounded by a wreath of flowers. The background features small shells, each one an inch and a half in size and done in four different shades of grey. This tapestry contains 42 different colours of wool. The authors have donated it to La Société Saint-Pierre and it is on permanent exhibition in the entrance of the Élizabeth Lefort Gallery.

In 1982, the Knights of Columbus—a Catholic society whose members are sworn to some secrecy, founded in New Haven (U.S.A.), with branches throughout North America—celebrated the centennial of their founding. To commemorate this anniversary, one of the Chéticamp members, Mr. Wilfred (à Anselme) Boudreau, decided to have the banner of the Knights hooked by Chéticamp artisans and then presented to the Council of the local chapter of the association. He wanted it to be especially well done so he asked Mr. Gérard Deveau to do it.

This banner, eight square feet in area with gold letters and a complex coat of arms on a black background, was stamped on canvas by Mr. Deveau, who also hooked the motifs and the letters. Mrs. Henriette Aucoin and Mrs. Marie-Rose Deveau hooked the background. The banner has gold woolen fringes;

it is very beautiful. It was presented to the Council of the Knights of Columbus at the official banquet of the centennial.

[See colour photos 13, 14 and 15.]

An artist in water colours, Mrs. Claire Guillemette-Lamirande from Ottawa, is renowned for her imaginative paintings with vivid distinct colours which lend themselves particularly well to the illustration of stories and legends. Her paintings are very well liked by children, and adults are reminded of their younger days by these paintings.

In 1981 Mrs. Lamirande and her husband, while visiting the Maritimes, stopped at Les Trois Pignons where they met Mr. and Mrs. Gérard Deveau. The latter showed them rugs which the couple had hooked and gave them a demonstration of rug hooking. Very enthusiastic about what she had seen, Mrs. Lamirande asked if they could reproduce in a tapestry one of her paintings, specifically that of the "Giant Lady of the Night," the story of Tit-Jean Quatorze from Antonine Maillet's book, *Pélagie-la-charrette*.[12] Mr. and Mrs. Deveau hesitated before accepting Mrs. Lamirande's request because the tapestry would be five square feet in area and would feature a giant lady with orange and red hair, with a yellow face in the midst of purple and red trees, etc. Gérard stamped the canvas; Annie-Rose dyed the wool in vivid colours. The two hooked the tapestry. The people and students of the courses in rug hooking were amazed by this kind of motif with its vivid colours, totally foreign to the style of Chéticamp hooked rugs. Annie-Rose, however, would interpret for them the meaning of the tapestry while telling them the story of Tit-Jean.

[See colour photo 33.]

When Mrs. Lamirande received her tapestry, she was so happy with it that she paid one hundred dollars more than the price agreed upon. This tapestry journeyed from one exhibition to the next during the whole summer of 1982.

Mrs. Lamirande has had four other tapestries made based on her paintings, illustrating the following tales: "Le Roi dupé par Tit-Jean," "Le Fou de la poule caille," "L'Homme du paradis," and "Gendron et le faux curé."[13] The artist is so satisfied with the work of Mr. and Mrs. Deveau that she does not want anybody else to work on the tapestries she orders.

In conclusion, it is fitting that we describe another rug which was made by Mr. and Mrs. Deveau. It measures twelve square feet in area and features the house where Father Charles Aucoin, c.j.m.—son of Moïse (à Séverin) Aucoin of Chéticamp—was born, as well as the barn which is no more and a large tree, rich in symbolism. The ten branches of the tree represent the ten years which Father Aucoin spent in Chéticamp; the countless leaves and their multiple colours represent the hundred thousand index cards which he has compiled on the genealogy of the families of the area. Finally the tree's six roots represent the six virtues which are part of Father Aucoin's character: determination, devotion, unselfishness, readiness to help, patriotism and enthusiasm.[14]

[See colour photo 25.]

Mr. and Mrs. Deveau have made many other beautiful rugs. They are passionately in love with this form of handcrafts. They continually try hard to create new designs and new projects which will contribute to the advancement of this art. They hope that one day they will see regular courses given in the stamping of designs, the dyeing of wool and the technique of hooking itself. Because of their knowledge and their energy, they have been the driving force for the creation of the Élizabeth Lefort Gallery at Les Trois Pignons, where the rugs of that great artist as well as other important tapestries are on permanent exhibition.

Finally, Mrs. Deveau has devoted four years to the research of the history associated with rug making in Chéticamp. The result of her work has been an illustrated album, which is on exhibition at the Élizabeth Lefort Gallery, and this book.

Other personalities

There would be personalities of another genre that would certainly be worthy of mention, such as people with a special talent to dye wool perfectly in multiple colours. Others could be mentioned for their ability to stamp a design on a canvas. Still others could be recognized because their devotion to the making of rugs has marked both their own lives and this particular form of handcraft. However, the dividing line between an expert in the field, and a person who is but remarkable in the field, is difficult to draw. For this reason two other personalities will be presented and will be used as examples.

Mrs. Marie-Louise Cormier (1929-   )

Marie-Louise Lefort, wife of Isidore (à Job) Cormier, is blessed with all the abilities outlined above. She has an unfailing devotion to rug making, and she excels at stamping designs on canvas and at dyeing wool. To top all this, she is also very good with the rug hook.

[See colour photo 17.]

Marie-Louise's devotion to the cause of the Coopérative artisanale, of which she was the first president, and to that organization's projects concerning rugs, will be discussed later in the book. Her name will be mentioned several times in connection with this topic.

Marie-Louise is especially adept at dyeing wool. When dyeing the wool, she is able to obtain with precision several tones and, from a basic colour, she can obtain five or six different shades of it. She is recognized as one of the best in Chéticamp where dyeing wool is concerned.

This special talent enables her to give her tapestries a unique, original and personal character.

She specializes in floral designs. Most ladies can reproduce the design of a flower using three or four colours, but Marie-Louise is able to reproduce a flower with seven or eight tones of the same colour, giving the flower a fresh-from-the-field look.

Since 1971, Marie-Louise has especially concentrated her efforts on stamping canvases for the various Chéticamp boutiques. These canvases, in turn, have then been hooked by other ladies. She has stamped as much as 700, even 800, yards of canvas in a year. In a year, she would also dye between 500 and 600 pounds of wool for the Coopérative artisanale. All that was an enormous amount of work.

Mrs. Luce-Marie Boudreau (1929-   )

Mrs. Luce-Marie (à Joseph-Athanase) Boudreau is renowned for the beautiful tapestries which she makes and for her unending devotion to the cause of this form of handcraft in Chéticamp.

Her most remarkable tapestries are without a doubt those featuring the coats of arms of Canada and the picturesque landscapes of Cape Breton, for example the "Presqu'île" and "La rivière à Lazare" at Cap Rouge. The tapestry featuring "La rivière à Lazare" measures 18 inches by 24 inches and was bought by a committee in charge of the Évangéline Festival and presented in the name of the Chéticamp citizens to the Prime Minister of Canada, the Honourable Pierre Elliot Trudeau, when he visited Chéticamp in 1971.

[See colour photo 16.]

Mrs. Boudreau also likes to reproduce abstract designs as well as flowers and even snowstorms. One of her tapestries represents a *suête* (south-east wind) which in the Chéticamp region sometimes reaches the intensity of a hurricane. It is a reproduction of a painting by her sister, Lucienne Deveau. The painting was done for a contest sponsored by Francis Coutelier when he gave visual arts courses in Chéticamp in 1970.

Her devotion to the handcraft of rugs and tapestries has certainly been manifested through her work at La Coopérative artisanale. She was elected president in 1966 and later managed the Coopérative with great success.

A good administrator, with the help of Mr. Edmond Aucoin, then Manager of the Credit Union, she began by establishing a well organized system of finances and accounts for the Coopérative. She ordered jute canvas in large rolls which she then cut into canvases to the dimension of the rugs to be made by local ladies. She also ordered wool in bulk. In the

117

earlier days of the Coopérative, she worked almost day and night to obtain and supply the required materials to the clients, to collect their rugs, and to try to find buyers for them.

Twice a year she took part in the national exhibitions of handcrafts in Toronto—National Fall Gift Show in September, and National Spring Gift Show in February. She also participated in the annual Halifax Atlantic Craft Show—an exhibition held for all the Maritime Provinces. She was a member of the Nova Scotia Designer Craftsmen. Finally she maintained constant contact with the societies which could help her promote this form of handcrafts in Chéticamp.

In 1976 Mrs. Boudreau obtained from the Federal Government a grant which made it possible to expand and improve the building which houses the Coopérative artisanale. She also obtained from the Provincial Government the first grants which made possible rug hooking courses in Chéticamp.

Finally, in everybody's opinion, Mrs. Boudreau

Mrs. Luce-Marie Boudreau

was responsible for a great part of the success and expansion of the activities of the Coopérative artisanale. She figures among the women who have especially devoted themselves to the craft of hooked rugs in Chéticamp. [See in the following chapter, "The Boutiques," the prodigious expansion of La Coopérative artisanale de Chéticamp ltée., under the management of Mrs. Luce-Marie Boudreau.]

1. Daniel Aucoin, *Le Courrier*, Cape Breton Edition, June 15, 1983, p. 1.

2. *Arizona Register*, "Artist in wool lives in Phoenix," Friday, December 8, 1961.

3. "Reflected Beauty" by Margaret L. Perry, published in the *Family Herald*, March 9, 1961, p. 38.

4. "Artist in wool lives in Phoenix," *Arizona Register*, December 8, 1961.

5. *The Oran*, Inverness, N.S., May 21, 1981, p. 6.

6. *Handcrafts*, Halifax, N.S., April 1960, p. 2.

7. *Ibid.*

8. "Portraits in wool," *Arizona Journal*, Sunday, March 4, 1962, p. 4.

9. Personal notes of Mr. Kenneth Hansford.

10. "Reflected Beauty—In the skilled hands of this dedicated Cape Breton artist," by Margaret L. Perry, *The Family Herald*, March 9, 1961.

11. *Le Courrier*, Cape Breton Edition, Wednesday, August 17, 1983, p. 6.

12. Antonine Maillet, *Pélagie-la-charrette*, éd. Leméac, Montréal, 1979, pp. 305 to 311.

13. Germain Lamieux, *Les vieux m'ont conté*, éd. Bellarmin, Montréal, 1981, T-2, pp. 55-61, 32-50, 79-90, 91-97.

14. This rug was presented to Father Aucoin on October 29, 1983. See *Le Courrier*, Cape Breton Edition, November 9, 1983, p. 1.

CHAPTER 12

The Boutiques

The tourist industry was slow to develop in Chéticamp even with the opening, around 1936, of the Cabot Trail, the highway which winds its way through the Highlands of Cape Breton. The first bus tour came to Chéticamp in 1940. Since that year, the number of tourists visiting Chéticamp has steadily increased. Facilities have been developed to accommodate them, such as hotels, motels, restaurants, etc. Tourism quickly developed into an important source of revenue for this Acadian village.

The tourists showed an immediate interest in Chéticamp hooked rugs. They would visit the distributing agents to buy these rugs and often to order some with special designs. Soon after this display of interest, the ladies who had hooked rugs realized that the most likely way to sell their rugs was to offer them for sale in the stores where the tourists usually stopped. Slowly, handcraft boutiques, specializing in hooked rugs, began to appear along the main highway in Chéticamp.

The Acadian Inn Restaurant

In 1924, Mr. Marcellin (à Médée) Aucoin opened the Acadian Inn along the Chéticamp harbour. This restaurant was to quickly acquire a good reputation for its fine cuisine and its friendly atmosphere. In 1935, the Acadian Inn was expanded to accommodate more tourists overnight. In that same year, Mr. Aucoin's daughter Adelaïde married Joseph (à John)

Acadian Inn in Chéticamp

Chiasson and both started working in the restaurant.

Mr. Aucoin, very early on, accepted that the local ladies leave their hooked rugs on consignment at the restaurant, for sale to tourists. He was the first to do so. Up to that time, the rugs had been sold in individual homes or in the living rooms of the distributing agents.

Every Sunday, after mass, the ladies who had left rugs to be sold would go into the restaurant to find out if their merchandise had been sold. This would cause Mr. Aucoin to waste valuable time that was needed to attend to the tourists. To avoid this scramble, he placed in front of the door a blackboard on which he wrote the name of the ladies who had sold rugs. The ladies who had been successful stopped to claim their money; the less fortunate ones didn't need to bother.

Many rugs and tapestries were sold at the Acadian Inn. In its earlier days the Acadian Inn would close for the winter. Adelaïde would then attend to having the tourists' orders for special rugs filled. Her mother Nanette and her aunt Antoinette would spend most of their time working on those special orders, but they could not cope with the demand. To be able to fill all these special orders, Adelaïde had to have recourse to the services of several ladies of the area.

As was mentioned earlier, Antoinette Deveau *[see page 68]*, victim of poliomyelitis, courageously earned her living by making hooked rugs. One day, three men stopped at the Acadian Inn: a Mr. Cumins was in a wheelchair, another could walk only with the help of a cane, and the third was the other two's chauffeur. As was her custom with all the tourists, Adelaïde talked with them for a long time, answering all their questions about Chéticamp, about how the people earned their living and about the business of rug making. During the conversation, she mentioned her aunt Antoinette. Mr. Cumins asked to go visit her. He was astonished by her work. This Mr. Cumins was one of the directors of the Canadian Association for Paraplegics. A few weeks later Antoinette was the happy recipient of a wheelchair and a sewing machine, donations of that association.

Marie LeLièvre's Hooked Rugs Boutique

Mrs. Marie (à Philippe) LeLièvre (1889-1968) was a courageous woman who liked to help the people around her. Even if she did not have that much education—only grade two level—and even if she did not know how to hook a rug, in 1937 she launched herself into the rug making business. She was the first to open a rug boutique in Chéticamp. Up to that time, the women would sell their rugs at home or at the Acadian Inn's restaurant. Her boutique was situated by the roadside at the southwest entrance to the village.

Mrs. Marie LeLièvre

Mrs. LeLièvre did not favour the practice of shipping rugs which had been ordered by boutiques outside the village. She believed that the tourists who had found these rugs elsewhere would not bother to come to Chéticamp.

Mrs. Élizabeth (à Onésime) Muise would hook many rugs for Mrs. LeLièvre. Mrs. Muise and Marguerite-Marie Chiasson would also stamp designs on canvases which Mrs. LeLièvre had made into rugs by other ladies. As mentioned before, Mrs. LeLièvre had designed the motif for a rug called "The Tree of Life," which had been stamped on canvas by Marguerite-Marie and had afterwards become renowned because in 1976 it was presented as a gift from the Province of Nova Scotia to Queen Elizabeth II.

[See colour photo 6.]

Mrs. LeLièvre wanted to help the people earn some money from their rugs. To help out the people in greater need, she even paid them for their rugs before they were made.

In 1967, Mrs. LeLièvre retired after thirty years in a flourishing business. She died the following year.

Her daughter, Marie-Thérèse, wife of Séverin LeBlanc, took over her mother's business. In 1969 she bought Charlie (à Hélore) Deveau's old house which she had moved next to the boutique. She managed to find beds, chairs, chests, utensils and whatever else was necessary to furnish this house as it would have been in earlier times. Tourists entering her store were invited to visit, free of charge, this veritable museum called the "Old Acadian House."

One year, some of the older girls attending the regional school of Chéticamp gave guided tours of the museum. Dressed in Évangéline costumes, they gave demonstrations on how to card and spin wool and how to hook a rug. The tourists were very interested, but unfortunately the project was discontinued the following year.

Marie-Thérèse ran the business successfully for ten years. Numerous tourists visited her boutique and she also received many orders at large for rugs.

When Marie-Thérèse gave up her rug business, her brother Alfred, who ran a grocery store next door, converted his store into a handcraft and rug boutique. The latter closed in 1983. The rug boutique started by Mrs. Marie LeLièvre and run as a family business by her children lasted for a period of forty-six years.

"Le Foyer du souvenir" boutique

Le Foyer du souvenir

In 1947, Mr. Louis-Philippe Chiasson rented a small building situated at the harbour. This building was the former house of Placide (à Simon) Leblanc. In 1947, it belonged to Willie (à Charles) Roach. He converted it into a souvenir boutique. He named it "Le Foyer du souvenir"; it was the second boutique in Chéticamp to offer hooked rugs.

Mr. Chiasson stayed in the business for two years and the following year sold the business to Mrs. Florence (à Job) Deveau.

She also was an accomplished rug maker but she could not fill the orders of the tourists nor the orders coming from other parts of the country.

Mrs. Deveau would create her own designs and have them made into rugs by other women. She also attended many exhibitions from where she returned with numerous orders for rugs.

After her death in 1960, her son Freddie and his wife

Mrs. Florence Deveau

Patricia ran the business successfully for another twenty years. By 1980 the business had become too taxing, so they closed the boutique and sold the building to an insurance broker [Simon-Pierre Boudreau] who converted it into a business office.

Flora's Boutique

In 1958 Albert (à Alphée) Boudreau and Marie-Flora [daughter of Pitt (à Hubert) Poirier], his wife, bought from

Flora's Boutique

Tom Lefort a small grocery store situated on a byway at Point Cross, to the west of Chéticamp.

Situated at the entrance to the village, this boutique dealing in rugs was an immediate success. The grocery aspect of the business soon had to be abandoned to make room for the rug business. Even if the boutique was opened for the summer only, that is during the tourist season, the rug business continued beyond that season. Marie-Flora and her neighbour Antoinette Lefort [see page 82] worked after the seasonal closing, making rugs for the following summer and also filling orders which came from other parts of the country. They could not cope with the work, and Marie-Flora had to hire several women to help. Antoinette Lefort specialized in stamping the designs on the canvases.

The volume of business underwent a constant growth. In 1977 it became necessary to hire a second person to work in the boutique for the summer (Marie-Mai Aucoin), and in 1978 an extension had to be added to the boutique. Besides the addition, the owner also took advantage of this occasion to give the renovated boutique a pleasant and attractive look. The building was given a new look both outside and inside; a parking lot was expanded and paved with asphalt so that it could accommodate automobiles and buses. A freshly painted fishing boat with two masts bearing the Acadian Flag was set up on the grounds.

The following year (1979) the volume of business increased so that two more persons had to be hired to work in the boutique. It was then that Marie-Flora, who had become widowed and who was overwhelmed by the extent of the business, appealed to her daughter Marie, and her husband René Lefort, to take over the business. They left Montréal where they were living at the time and came home to manage the boutique and continue the business.

This store, which features rugs and tapestries, is without a doubt the most pleasant one in Chéticamp due to its exterior look, and the quality and artistic display of its merchandise. It is not really surprising that in 1982 the Provincial Tourist Association chose Flora's Boutique as "the best one in all of Cape Breton."

La Coopérative artisanale de Chéticamp ltée

It was mentioned previously that certain supporters of the cooperative movement had suggested to their friends, Mr. Louis-Léo Boudreau and his wife Marie-Stella, to start a cooperative operation for the production and sale of rugs.

This idea was quickly realized. In 1963, a group of women met with Marie-Stella to study the possibility of founding such an organization. Resource personnel, such as Mr. Joseph T. Chiasson of the St. Francis Xavier University Adult Education Department, Mr. Rémi Chiasson of the Extension Department of the same university, and Messrs. Churchill and Adair Stewart of the Province's Department of Industry and Commerce, were invited to these study sessions. After many meetings and much study, it was decided to start a cooperative association which was named, according to Mr. Rémi Chiasson's suggestion, La Coopérative artisanale de Chéticamp ltée.

An administrative board[1] and a president[2] were nominated and the project was launched with much enthusiasm.

A constitution was drawn up and a provincial charter was obtained. What was needed now was a building somewhere at the harbour. At that time the firemen had just had a new fire

Coopérative artisanale of Chéticamp

station built to better suit their needs. The Coopérative artisanale bought the firemen's other property, renovated the building and opened their new boutique on June 15, 1964.

The members of the cooperative would leave their products on consignment at the boutique so that they could be sold to tourists. The Coopérative would keep a small percentage of the sales and would thus be able to finance its operation. Merchandise from non-members was also accepted under the same terms as for members.

In the beginning, only one person was paid a salary for working at the cooperative. The other members volunteered their services faithfully and enthusiastically. Marie-Stella Bourgeois and Marie-Louise Cormier made the billboards, painting the letters and the background scenes themselves.

In its first year of business, the boutique was visited by nearly four thousand tourists, and that number has been increasing ever since. Many companies which organize bus tours of the Cabot Trail add a visit to the Coopérative artisanale to their itinerary after having made their intentions known to the personnel of the cooperative.

This cooperative system is very efficient. It eliminates intermediaries between the buyers and the people who produce the rugs, allowing the producers more money for their efforts. The Coopérative has also been able to substantially increase the price of hooked rugs.

To make the boutique more attractive to tourists, it was decided in 1967 to add a small museum featuring items of interest associated with fishing and farming as well as tools which were used in the older days. As the business volume was increasing considerably, two more people had to be hired to work at the Coopérative.

In 1976, the boutique had to be expanded because of the crowds of tourists visiting and because of the greater amount of merchandise left on consignment. At this time a basement was also built and was turned into a small restaurant. The restaurant serves Acadian dishes of local origin featuring fish, homemade bread and pastries. All of the food served is cooked on the premises.

The small museum was also moved to the basement, and new items were added. In keeping with the nature of the boutique, a demonstration of the process by which wool is prepared is given, starting with the sheep and on to the finished product, the hooked rug. A ram with its wool and horns was stuffed by Marie-Stella Bourgeois. While tourists look on, a person demonstrates how to card and spin wool, works with the special hook, and shows the tourists how to hook a rug. A loom was also installed and is used to explain how rugs and drapes were woven out of *breillons*. Finally, Marie-Stella Bourgeois has dressed up a mannequin as an old woman of years ago, in the process of knitting.

To add diversity to the museum, Mr. Alphonse Saulnier has transformed a corner into a chapel. He has added an altar with old style candle holders. He has also created three life-size statues: one of a bishop, one of a priest and one of an altar boy—all wearing the vestments in use in an earlier era.

In 1983, this handcraft cooperative comprised twenty-five

members. From its modest beginnings with only one person on salary, the staff has had to be gradually increased.

The Coopérative artisanale has the greatest turnover in Chéticamp in the business of handcrafts. It is a regular exhibitor at the fairs in Toronto and the one in Halifax. Representatives from everywhere, especially the owners of handcraft boutiques, attend these fairs. The Coopérative sells many tapestries at these shows. The many orders which its representatives bring back from these exhibitions, plus the ones which arrive regularly from all over Canada by mail, provide work for a large number of people.

The Coopérative artisanale has become an internationally known boutique with considerable renown. In fact, if a public organization wishes to have a special tapestry made for a definite purpose, it usually calls on the Coopérative. Here is one example from many. When Parks Canada built a historical site at the Lefebvre Monument of Memramcook in order to illustrate the survival of Acadians—the opening took place in 1982—it commissioned the Coopérative artisanale to produce a tapestry depicting the Dispersion of the Acadians.

The design was done by Miss Jocelyne Doiron of Moncton, New Brunswick. Mrs. Marie-Louise Cormier was given the task of dyeing the wool in 42 different shades of colour. And under the supervision of Mrs. Luce-Marie Boudreau, manager of the Coopérative, four ladies [Mrs. Sadie Roach, Mrs. Ethel Deveau, Mrs. Marie-Adèle Poirier and Mrs. Marie-Louise Cormier] made this 30-square-foot tapestry, which required 657,000 loops with the hook and 725 hours of work. This magnificent tapestry now has a permanent place in the historical monument of Memramcook. *[See colour photo 11.]*

By itself, the Coopérative artisanale is an important industry of Chéticamp. Its success is the result of much volunteer work by its members as well as their great devotion and dynamism.

Edna's Gift Shop

In 1965 or 1966, Mrs. Edna (à Freddie) Deveau, daughter

of Moïse (à Charlo) Romard, bought Mr. Hubert (à Laurent) LeBlanc's house and converted a part of it into a rug boutique.

Edna herself made some very beautiful rugs and she bought quite a few from women in Chéticamp so that she could fill the orders which she received. After ten successful years in the business, she had to close down the boutique because of ill health.

Hooked Rugs of Clothilde and Henri Bourgeois

In 1971, Mr. Henry Bourgeois and his wife Clothilde bought Sandy (à Polite) Boudreau's property situated in the Redman region and converted the garage into a handcraft boutique. Closed for the following year, this store opened its doors in 1975 and continued its business activities up to 1979. The closing of this boutique was due to its owners moving to another part of Chéticamp. Clothilde is still making hooked rugs which she sells to the boutique Warp and Woof owned by Mrs. Flinn of Chester.

Jean's Gift Shop

Mrs. Jeannie (à Joseph) Poirier has always hooked rugs which she sold in the various boutiques in Chéticamp. In 1973 she had part of her house, situated in the region of Chéticamp known as La Prairie, converted into a handcraft boutique, and since then she sells her own rugs and the rugs of her friends. Her boutique is open from the first of May to the first of November. Her store abounds with beautiful rugs and magnificent souvenirs. Jeannie is always present to greet the tourists with friendliness. In 2004, Jean's Handcrafts was sold to Lola LeLièvre and Annette Larade.

"Jean's Handcrafts" boutique

Bella Poirier's Hooked Rugs

Bella Poirier, wife of Henri Lefort, is a very active business-woman in the field of hooked rugs.

She began her business modestly in 1962 in her own house with only one dollar in cash. Her first customer, Father Champlain from Rimouski, bought a rug which he paid for by cheque.

She immediately sent her son to deposit the cheque at the bank, for she might need funds in her account when dealing with her next customer.

From that point on, Bella has managed successive boutiques. In

Bella Poirier's Hooked Rugs

1966 she rented a building from Wilfred (à Charlie) Aucoin for the purpose of setting up a boutique. In 1968 she moved into Mrs. Job (à Lubin) Muise's small store, and the following year she set up shop in Marie-Thérèse LeBlanc's boutique.

Gradually, because of many trips to attend exhibitions or to give courses in rug hooking, she gave up managing a boutique. However, she still buys hooked rugs to fulfill the requests which she receives from the many people she has met through her travels.

Mrs. Lefort has taken part in many exhibitions outside Chéticamp and often her kiosk has won first prize. In 1965, she had the honour of being chosen by the federal Department of Industry and Commerce to represent the rug industry at an exhibition of North American handcrafts held in Grand Rapids, Michigan.

The Acadian Lighthouse

Marie-Jeannette, wife of Joseph (à Charles) Gaudet, has always hooked rugs which she would sell either at Mrs. Marie Deveau's boutique or at the other boutiques in Chéticamp. The

The Acadian Lighthouse

fruit of her work had for a long time supplied her with a modest income which was indispensable for the support of her family.

Marie-Jeannette makes very beautiful rugs. She is especially known for her tapestries which feature the coat of arms of Canada. A Mrs. Merchant from Mahone Bay, Nova Scotia, who managed a handcraft boutique herself, one day happened upon one of these tapestries at Mrs. Marie Deveau's. She wanted to meet the author personally. At that time, Marie-Jeannette was burdened by illness and poverty in her family. Mrs. Merchant consoled her and ordered several tapestries, among them one featuring the coat of arms of Canada. One of these coat of arms of Canada tapestries is now in Denmark in the office of Oland Beer; another is at Mr. Robert Stanfield's house, former Premier of Nova Scotia and leader of the Canadian Progressive Conservative Party; a thirty-six-square-foot tapestry is in one of the Canadian National Railway stations.

The bonds of friendship which develop between buyers and the people who make rugs are outstanding. One year, much to her sorrow, Marie-Jeannette foresaw that she would not have the means to buy Christmas gifts for her children. She confided her plight to Mrs. Merchant who sent her 125 dollars to help her.

Thanks to the publicity provided by Mrs. Merchant and to the quality of her product, Marie-Jeannette saw the day that she could not supply the demand she had for rugs, so she started buying them from other Chéticamp ladies.

In 1977 she decided to convert the small office of her

husband, who in the meantime had become an entrepreneur, into a rug boutique. The success that she had that first year enabled her to start another boutique, bigger and original in design—that of a lighthouse—which she appropriately named the Acadian Lighthouse.

Le Gabion

In 1978, another souvenir boutique which also sold hooked rugs was opened at l'Anse-du-bois-marié. This boutique was especially remarkable because of its structure which in effect was a large lobster trap. Its owner was Mr. Simon-Pierre Boudreau.

Le Gabion

Chéticamp Gift Shop

Finally, Mr. Joseph Larade opened, in 1981, a new rug boutique at the harbour in the old grocery store which once belonged to Mr. Herbert LeBoutillier. Two people worked there as sales clerks and also gave interested tourists demonstrations on how to hook a rug.

•

All of these boutiques provide jobs for many employees and make it possible for a great number of people to sell their hooked rugs as well as other forms of handcrafts, which bring to Chéticamp an annual revenue of half a million dollars.

Chéticamp Gift Shop

1. An interim administration board met in the basement of the Church on July 26, 1963. It consisted of Mrs. Marie-Hélène Maillet, Mrs. Ethel Deveau, Mrs. Bella Lefort, Mrs. Agnès Larade, Mrs. Élizabeth Deveau and Mrs. Marie-Louise Cormier. On August 9th of the same year, at a meeting held at the home of Mrs. Marie-Stella Bourgeois, Mrs. Marie-Louise Cormier was elected President, Mrs. Bella Lefort, Vice-President, Mrs. Élizabeth Deveau, Secretary, and Mrs. Ethel Deveau, Mrs. Agnès Larade, Mrs. Thérèse Bourgeois and Mrs. Rhéa Poirier were elected as advisors.

2. Marie-Louise Cormier. Her successors have been: Luce-Marie Boudreau, Annie-Rose Deveau, Hilda Chiasson, Marie Larade, Thérèse Aucoin, Marguerite Doucet, Emilie Dithurbide.

CHAPTER 13

New Initiatives and Perspectives for the Future

The tremendous expansion of the hooked rug industry is such that every family in Chéticamp has some interest in it and a large number of people are directly involved in it. Rug making has become an integral part of community life in this Acadian village.

With many people, hooked rugs are the most frequent topic of conversation and maybe even their dreams. New ideas frequently spring up—on how to take advantage of the tourists' infatuation for rugs, on how to improve the finished product, or on how to show rugs off to advantage. This last chapter will explore some of the promising ideas and some interesting achievements which illustrate very well the constant energy which is associated with this remarkable form of handcraft.

Rug making kits

In 1965, Marie-Louise Cormier and her husband Isidore made available for sale in Chéticamp boutiques small hooked rug kits. These consist of a pre-stamped canvas, a hook and wool dyed in the colours necessary for the design. Tourists who like rugs and tapestries, and who are interested by the demonstrations on how to hook a rug, are very often happy to be able to buy a small kit which will enable them to try hooking a rug for themselves when they have returned home.

Courses on how to hook rugs

The quality of Chéticamp hooked rugs and tapestries, as well as the interest shown by the tourists in demonstrations given on how to hook a rug, have created an awareness, locally and elsewhere, of the need to give courses in this particular field of handcrafts.

From the beginning of this industry in Chéticamp, the teaching of this craft was done on a one-on-one basis, and no formal instruction was given to groups of people before 1972.

Mrs. Bella (à Henri) Lefort was the first to take the initiative in this form of training. Each year since 1972, she has given several courses which last two or three days each. She has toured the province of Nova Scotia, teaching courses in Louisbourg, Sydney, Glace Bay, Saint Peter's, Port Hawkesbury, Mabou, Antigonish and Saint-Joseph-du-Moine. She has even taught a six-week course in Chéticamp itself. She has also taught a course in Cape Saint George, Newfoundland; and in 1965 while attending an exhibition in Grand Rapids, Michigan, from October 11 to October 23, her demonstration on how to hook rugs was the equivalent of a genuine course on the subject. *[See page 131.]*

The Department of Culture and Recreation each year used to have funds available for adult education. The funds allotted were destined for courses in various subjects depending on the local needs.

In Saint-Joseph-du-Moine, the neighbouring parish of Chéticamp, some of the women indicated their interest in a course in hooked rugs. They managed to obtain a grant from the Department for that purpose. These courses were taught two years in a row in 1982 and 1983. The course was taught one night a week for a period of ten weeks by Mrs. Rita (à Wilfred) Chiasson, an accomplished hooked rug artisan.

For the course to be available, tools of the trade were

necessary. The first year Mr. Gérard Deveau of Chéticamp supplied hooks and frames to the students who didn't have their own. Mr. Deveau also gave his support by stamping designs on the small canvases which were to be hooked during the course. The following year, 1983, the group was better organized and managed to be self-sufficient.

It is in Chéticamp, however, that more important and more organized courses have been available since a few years. In this case, the funding for the courses is also from grants from the Department of Culture and Recreation of the province.

The initiative for the courses came from Mrs. Luce-Marie Boudreau, President of the Coopérative artisanale, whose devotion to the rug making industry and to the Coopérative knows no boundaries. She obtained a grant in 1975.

Organizing these courses was the responsibility of Mrs. Gérard Deveau *[see pages 109 to 116]*, Annie-Rose. The courses were taught at the Coopérative artisanale and Mrs. Luce-Marie Boudreau helped Mrs. Deveau, especially by stamping the canvases. The first course was attended by a group of fifteen women and lasted for eight months, from September to April, on the basis of one night a week.

In 1976 Mr. Gerard Deveau assisted his wife, helping her to teach this course, and they have continued to do so each year since. As early as 1976 they taught a course not only in Chéticamp but also a similar one in Margaree. Sixty-six women and girls followed the course. In 1977 and 1978, two courses were taught in Chéticamp and one was given in Belle-Côte (Margaree). In 1980 the Department of Culture and Recreation cut back on the grants which had so easily been obtained from the Department, and funding for these courses was no longer available. An appeal was launched to the Secretary of State in Ottawa and the funds necessary to continue these courses were granted. That year, the course was taught at Les Trois Pignons.

Up to this point the courses had been sponsored by the Coopérative artisanale, but in 1981 La Société Saint-Pierre assumed the sponsorship and has since made it its concern to obtain the necessary grants from the Secretary of State.

These courses have proven to be very successful and are becoming more extensive. In 1982, 1983 and 1984 they gave two courses each year in Chéticamp, and a course was also taught in another Acadian village of Cape Breton, namely Petit-de-Grat.

Mr. and Mrs. Deveau devoted themselves to the teaching of these courses, approaching them with fervour and enthusiasm. Mr. Deveau supplied the students with hooks and lent them frames which he made himself.

Their courses covered all the practical knowledge necessary to hook beautiful rugs: how to use various tools, how to dye the wool in the various shades necessary, how to stamp a canvas, and finally how to use the hook starting from the simpler stitches on to the more difficult ones.

The students began with a canvas six square inches in area and reproduced on it a flower with a few leaves. They learned how to blend colours, how to reproduce round shapes, oblique lines, etc. The course ended with a more difficult design, a landscape featuring various colours, for example.

These courses were formerly closed with a social gathering where students expressed their heartfelt gratitude to their teachers, Annie-Rose and Gérard Deveau.

Since 1986, Marie-Claire Doucet teaches two rug hooking courses every year. The first one starts in mid October and ends in mid December, while the other is from early January to the end of March. There are usually 10 to 12 people who participate in each course.

These courses are of great importance for maintaining the exceptional quality of Chéticamp hooked rugs. The success and future expansion of the rug making industry, in fact, depend essentially on the quality of the finished product. If the quality of the rugs and tapestries were to deteriorate, their reputation and markets would be quickly ruined. The quality of these rugs and tapestries, already world famous, will be maintained because of courses taught by competent people in this kind of handcrafts.

[See colour photos 30 and 31.]

New horizons

The French and English departments of both radio and television of the C.B.C. for the Maritime Provinces have already produced several programs *[see page 79]* about this form of handcrafts in Chéticamp. In 1981, it was the turn of television from Saint-Pierre and Miquelon and also France.

That year, the Tourist Bureau of Saint-Pierre and Miquelon sent a team to shoot a film on Chéticamp and especially on the hooked rugs and their history. This film was televised first in the Islands of Saint-Pierre and Miquelon and then in France in the same year.

During the filming, Mr. Jean-Charles Girardin of the Tourist Bureau of those Islands, as well as his team, were so filled with wonder by the extraordinary quality of the product that they arranged with La Société Saint-Pierre to organize a tour for a group of rug makers to visit the Islands of Saint-Pierre and Miquelon and to set up an exhibition there. The tour turned out to be very agreeable and the exhibition was a success.

The group was welcomed by the Prefect of Saint-Pierre and interviewed on television.

The group also toured the islands and was warmly received everywhere they went. The group consisted of Mr. Yvon Deveau, General Manager of La Société Saint-Pierre, and his wife, Mr. and Mrs. Gérard Deveau, Mrs. Henriette Aucoin and Mrs. Marie-Rose Deveau.

There was a short exhibition of rugs at Miquelon which the whole population attended, and another one, for a longer period, at Saint-Pierre, which was as successful as the other. The local residents were very interested in this form of handcrafts hereto unknown in these Islands. The people were especially interested in having some of the ladies from Chéticamp come to the Islands and teach courses on how to hook rugs.

Mr. Girardin and the Prefect of Saint-Pierre even suggested that an exhibition of Chéticamp rugs be held in Paris with the possibility of opening up a market in France. Even if today (1983) these projects have not been realized, they are still being studied and are interesting prospects for the future.

Jamac Creations

Fabrics which would be hooked in the same manner as rugs, that is made with wool and a piece of burlap, could possibly be used in a multitude of ways. A little imagination and study of market possibilities could lead to the creation of other products which would be original, artistic and commercially viable.

The idea has already taken root. A seamstress, Mrs. Jeannine Aucoin, already in the sewing business with her workshop called Aux Quatre Épingles, and a rug maker, Mrs. Marie-Claire Doucet, formed a partnership and started Jamacs Creations, the main purpose of which is to create new hooked products. This name is made up from "Ja" for Jeannine and "Mac" for Marie-Claire, thus "Jamac."

As prototypes, they have produced a purse or handbag, a case for eyeglasses, a jewellery box, a lampshade, a vest and even a coat. The ideas for other products are unlimited.

The exhibition of these samples which they held in Halifax brought them many encouraging and promising comments.

Their hope is to start a workshop where several ladies would work, some preparing the wool in the desired colours, others creating the designs, and others hooking the products.

Launching such a project requires tenacity, time and money. It is, however, a serious project which has great possibilities for this form of handcrafts in the future.

These ideas are not totally new. For a long time, some Chéticamp women have been producing, in this manner, handbags, chair seats, and lately cases for eyeglasses and even bookmarks.

Projects aimed at producing larger rugs

The rugs produced today are not as large as they have been

in the past. It was already mentioned that Miss Burke would regularly commission large rugs, each more than one hundred square feet in area *[see pages 45 to 52]*. It is true that these larger rugs did not cost her much at that time, less than a dollar per square foot. It is also true that she found buyers for these rugs who paid handsomely. An example is the rug bought in Chéticamp for one hundred and fourteen dollars and sold to Henry Ford for four thousand dollars.

At this rate, it would still be profitable to make large rugs and doubtless there would still be buyers, be they important houses, societies, hotels or rich people who would be interested in acquiring these original and exclusive tapestries.

Mr. and Mrs. Gérard Deveau dream of rediscovering a market which would have a demand for these larger rugs. The sale of one of these large rugs based on its value would give the women who produced it a reasonable hourly salary and not one which is based on a square foot of work. It is worth noting that while the buyer thinks that he is paying dearly for the rugs, he is buying the product of a slow process which requires many hours of work and which in reality adds up to a relatively low hourly wage. It is hoped that with such a project some kind of cooperative formula, eliminating the need for agents, could be arrived at.

If the project of producing larger rugs could be realized, it would bring about an expansion of, and add a new dimension to, the rug making industry.

Project for a workshop on how to dye wool

The handcraft of rug making has become an important industry in Chéticamp, as has been stated previously, and will continue to be so and to grow, provided that the quality of the product is maintained at a high level. The tourists' infatuation with the rugs, which presently makes them very fashionable, represents a potential danger for the industry. It is tempting for the rug makers to produce rugs at a faster rate, motivated by fast money, and therefore sacrifice quality. The success of the industry is directly related to the quality of its product. If the latter diminishes in quality, the demand will lessen. Recently, several artisans have started using vinegar as a fixative in the wool-dyeing process, with the result that the rugs are fading more easily, which is not the case with wool dyed with sulfuric acid as a fixative. The choice of dye has to be studied also; it is important that top quality dye be used.

Faced with a possible inferior technique of dyeing wool and an increasing volume of rugs produced, the Chéticamp rug making industry is in urgent need of a workshop on how to best dye wool. This workshop should feature the most modern equipment such as an electrically heated vat, equipment which is calibrated so that the exact amount of dye required to give a specific shade of colour can be measured, this having to be possible for any shade of colour. The workshop would have to teach how to make any shade of colour permanent by the use of sulfuric acid as a fixative, and all these desired qualities in the colour of the wool should be able to be reproduced at will.

This workshop is of great importance to the people who have the future of the industry at heart. Accordingly, La Société Saint-Pierre, the Coopérative artisanale, and dedicated individuals such as Mr. and Mrs. Gérard Deveau and others, are working towards the actualization of this workshop. Hopefully, they will be successful. Such a successful workshop would be an important step towards the progress of rug and tapestry handcrafts and would be an important factor in guaranteeing the permanent quality of the product.

The Élizabeth Lefort Gallery

The rug boutiques in Chéticamp display their merchandise to their best advantage, but very seldom are they successful, in a special way, of bringing out the quality and value of their hooked rugs. Furthermore, when these rugs are bought, they disappear with their owners.

La Société Saint-Pierre, which has as one of its main goals

to promote Acadian culture, found it regrettable that some of those tapestries which made Chéticamp renowned were forever lost to that village. La Société Saint-Pierre also did not want some of Élizabeth Lefort's most valuable tapestries which she was keeping in her collection, as well as others which were produced by other artisans and which had historical value, to disappear. The Société reached the conclusion that a gallery to exhibit these works was essential and decided to set up such a gallery. On November 19, 1981, La Société Saint-Pierre reached an agreement with Élizabeth Lefort and her husband Kenneth Hansford, which enabled the society to take over twenty of this great artist's most beautiful tapestries.

This exceptional acquisition opened the door for a grant from Employment and Immigration Canada, according to its policy of community development, for the construction of the gallery. A new wing was added to Les Trois Pignons which was to become the Élizabeth Lefort Gallery. The official opening was held on August 2, 1983, during the Acadian festival called l'Escaouette.

The Élizabeth Lefort collection comprises many of her large tapestries, described in previous chapters [see pages 100 to 109], among which are "The Canadian Centennial," and "The History of the Presidents of the United States." Also featured is the religious series which comprises "The Nativity," "Jesus as an Adolescent," "Calvary" and "The Resurrection." There are also tapestries of important contemporary figures such as Her Majesty Queen Elizabeth II, The Honourable Lester Pearson, Mrs. Jacqueline Kennedy, the first seven American astronauts, and Élizabeth Lefort herself. Finally, the exhibition features two scenes, one representing the first settlers of the region and the other a landscape featuring deer. The Gallery also has beautiful photographs of tapestries which represent other important personalities.

The Gallery also exhibits a *breillon* rug, with a design by the Moïse Aucoin family [see page 28] and rugs once owned by Mrs. MacFarland [see pages 29 to 32] which are splendid souvenirs of the '30s. Also featured are "The Tree of Life" by Marie and Joseph-Léo Muise, and finally an impressive tapestry by Mrs. Antoinette Lefort *[see pages 82 to 84]* of the Pierced Rock at Cap Rouge, a part of Chéticamp expropriated by the Cape Breton Highlands National Park. It is planned to add to this collection, in time, other important tapestries and souvenirs.

From the very first year of its opening, the gallery has been visited by numerous tourists, sometimes as many as four hundred a day. A competent guide is present to greet the visitors and to explain to them the details of each tapestry, such as the number of colours and loops necessary for the artist to produce such a beautiful and delicate work of art made from ordinary wool.

Invariably, after such a guided tour the tourists ask for more information on how such a rug is actually made. In anticipation of such questions, a piece of canvas mounted on a frame can be found at the end of the tour. The guide then proceeds to give a demonstration of how a hooked rug is made.

The Élizabeth Lefort Gallery is a very important supplement to the hooked rug and tapestry handcrafts of Chéticamp.

Finally, the projects and their creations illustrate very much the ongoing vitality of this handcraft and are a good sign of its promising future.

Conclusion

This account of the hooked rugs and tapestries of Chéticamp had to be limited to the highlights which illustrate the development of this handcraft over more than a century and, more particularly, in the last fifty years when it experienced an astonishing progress. It is obvious, however, that hundreds of people who were not mentioned are constantly working at this craft, and it is the result of their efforts which each spring stocks the boutiques with rugs and tapestries in all sizes and designs imaginable.

As mentioned, what eventually happened to certain tapestries which are remembered from the past is unknown. No doubt, several other original and magnificent works were made in the village and forwarded to important people. However, there has been no record of this fact and people have forgotten about it. The following illustrates this fact. Alexander Graham Bell was the first man to have his airplane flown in Canada. The flight took place in Baddeck, Nova Scotia, on February 23, 1909. The plane was piloted by J. A. D. McCurdy. Around 1930 or 1931, some Chéticamp women made a 49-square-foot tapestry for the Baldwin family commemorating that 1909 flight. [The tapestry likely honours the fact that Baldwin was a member of the Aerial Experiment Association— a group made up of A. G. Bell, J. A. D. (Douglas) McCurdy, Casey Baldwin, Glenn Curtiss and Lt. Thomas Selfridge— funded by Mabel Bell and devoted to achieving manned flight.]

The present generation of Chéticamp does not remember the tapestry made in honour of this flight. La Société Saint-Pierre quite recently found the tapestry, which is still in very good condition and which is now in the possession of Casey Baldwin's descendants. The principal motif, done in what could

145

be likened to an Egyptian style, is a woman with wings launching herself into flight. The tapestry is called "The Spirit of Flight." *[See colour photo 32.]* It is a splendid tapestry featuring a style which is totally different from the usual style of rugs and tapestries made in Chéticamp.

Now that the history of this handcraft has become an important consideration, it is quite probable that other very valuable tapestries which have also been forgotten will be discovered.

No doubt, it would be wise to make sure that this handcraft has a future. The possibilities for its future are numerous, especially if people of vision make its development their mission. If the amount of rugs and tapestries produced is to increase while the level of quality is maintained, a workshop on how to dye wool is of primary importance.

The widespread reputation which this form of handcrafts presently enjoys is due firstly to the quality of the product and secondly to the publicity given to it by such people as Miss Lillian Burke, Mr. Kenneth Hansford, Mrs. Flinn of Chester, and others. It may be time to set up some kind of advertising agency which would contact prospective clients such as companies, major hotels and other institutions which could be interested in obtaining rare and original tapestries. This agency could also be on the watch for events in this country or in others which would be worth commemorating with tapestries.

There is also a possibility of rendering the motifs of these rugs and tapestries more artistic. The possibilities in this aspect of rug making are unlimited. While the present motifs are quite varied, should new artists use their imagination to create new and original designs for this form of handcrafts, the latter would be given a vital impulse which would ensure that it will not become a victim of stagnation.

In conclusion, with constant vigilance and properly oriented organization this unique handcraft, with its illustrious past, will not only maintain its present reputation but also ensure itself of a brilliant future.

Tribute to
Miss Lillian Burke

by Marian H. Bell Fairchild

It was many years ago that Lillian Burke first came to Cape Breton. It was while my father and mother, Mr. and Mrs. Alexander Graham Bell, were living, and they too loved "Burkie." We all did. She was so gay, so ready to throw herself enthusiastically into other people's interests, so able to bring out hidden abilities we didn't know we had.

I have never known anyone whose own talents were so completely useable. She could sit down at the piano with a group around her and improvise an accompaniment for anything they wanted to sing. Painting, drawing, modelling, working in metal— all her gifts could be called on at a moment's notice.

Half Irish and half Polish, she seemed to have picked out the most endearing and delightful qualities of both nationalities. No wonder she was a successful teacher in Washington and a successful occupational therapist with the American Army of Occupation in Germany both during and after the First World War.

It was in the summer of 1924 that we on Beinn Bhreagh first became concerned with hooked rugs. I had seen some rugs for sale in Florida that were so far inferior to many in Cape Breton farm houses that we thought it would be interesting to look into the situation.

Well, we found so many tucked away in cottage attics and closets as well as on floors, and the makers seemed so glad to think there might be money in them, that we gathered up enough to put on a sale in the Baddeck Public Library. Young and old from Beinn Bhreagh became saleswomen for a season. My memory is that we sold about $1,200 worth. A good many nice "mats" were left over, so many that Miss Burke volunteered to take them to New York and try to find a market for them. We like to think that in some way it was a

147

continuance of my mother's Cape Breton Home Industries of fifty years before.

The small rugs did not interest the big metropolitan decorators, but the workmanship did. Gradually Miss Burke was able to get orders for larger and larger rugs. She made the designs for the individual rooms and drew them out on the huge burlap foundations.

The French women of Cape Breton were more interested in hooking the big rugs than the Scotch women were; there was no gamble as to whether their work would sell or not, and they liked to set up a big frame that half a dozen people could work on at the same time. So naturally more and more of the industry was centred in Chéticamp, with Mrs. Marie Aucoin as Miss Burke's agent there. Burkie was a Catholic and she could speak French, which made things especially happy all around.

It was, sentimentally, a disappointment to find that vegetable dyes were not so satisfactory as chemical ones. Miss Burke got some fine German ones in the primary colors and the Chéticamp women showed extraordinary ability in blending them and getting an infinite variety of colors and shades.

The largest hooked rugs ever made were made there in Chéticamp and the most beautiful.

It was fun to drive around Chéticamp with Burkie in those days. She'd point out a new roof or the addition to a house—"Hooked rugs paid for that one," she'd say, "and for that one, too."

We'd stop at some door to inspect the hooking and out would come the children to greet her and of course she'd have a toy or a bit of ribbon or some candy for each one. And at summer's end she would give a party with little presents for all the workers and their children; presents she had picked up during the winter days in New York.

And then in 1939 the War came and Cape Breton Home Industries, like so many other civilian projects, collapsed. Miss Burke continued to come to Cape Breton every summer and to send sketches and a few orders to Chéticamp, but she could not give her whole time to it.

She took a position in the Psychiatric Institute in New York. Her studio, to which patients were sent as part of their treatment, became an important asset. As with the children of Beinn Bhreagh, she seemed able to make the patients want to paint and model. We had hoped she would be able to write up her experiences, because much of what she was doing was pioneer work, but it was not to be.

In the late winter of 1952 she had a stroke, and as spring came on, she died.

The inspiration she gave the women of Chéticamp will live, I hope, and I believe that for many years to come something of her, some quality of design or coloring, will show in the hooked mats of Chéticamp.

Father Anselme Chiasson (1911-2004)

Tribute to
Father Anselme Chiasson

by Donald Deschênes

I have known the work of Anselme Chiasson for more than 20 years, through his *Chansons d'Acadie* and *Chéticamp: History and Acadian Traditions*. Personally, I have known him for the last ten years. I have always been captured by the strength and simplicity of his work.

It is by his writing and his gestures that Anselme Chiasson communicates his pride in himself and what he is. His writing brings us to the point of re-evaluating who we are and what we have become as a community.

I've always admired his indestructible and unfailing confidence in Acadia, his faith in our future, influencing us to work collectively. There is nothing worse for Anselme Chiasson than a grudge, self-pity and lack of activity. In order to respect ourselves and to be respected, we have to accomplish certain tasks. We have to conquer the fear of others before trying to conquer the world. Life is too precious to vegetate. Anselme Chiasson is a good example of such fervour: always smiling, energetic, generous, enthusiastic, patient and impatient, demanding and conciliating, worrying and confident, daring and timid. These weaknesses as well as his strong points form his strength and vitality. I've known very few men at the age of 79 who would determine to reexamine their life's work and prepare it for publication, and who resume sketching and painting at 80, who drive their car with the passion of a young man of 20, who see this period as a rare commodity for self-fulfillment and not as a last resort waiting for death.

Father Anselme is an eminently sympathetic man who is very close to people. No wonder he has become a Capuchin. What is most astonishing about him is the fact that he's filled with wonder at the slightest thing. How often have I seen him arrive, from his height of almost two metres, this species of a giant, his wide smile, sharing with me his discoveries and talking about his many projects, his meetings and his readings.

Even if our society has civilized Anselme Chiasson, within reason, he always has the sense of wild freedom, perhaps a *suête* [a powerful southeast wind, typical on the west coast of Cape Breton] that blows next to his ear, always keeping him alert for the next adventure.

Donald Deschênes
Centre franco-ontarien de folklore
Sudbury, Ontario
1994

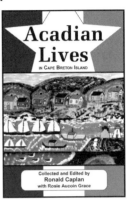

CONTINUED ON NEXT PAGE

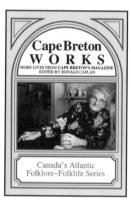